THAN SHWE'S

BURMA

DIANE ZAHLER

TF
CB TWENTY-FIRST CENTURY BOOKS   MINNEAPOLIS

For Jan and Stan

Acknowledgments:
Many thanks to the following: Peter Zahler, for his knowledge of tigers;
Kathy Zahler, for finding and sending invaluable information; Philip Sicker,
for reading every word and improving many of them; and especially Grace
Hasenbush, for her amazing recollections of Burma

Consultant: U Kyaw Win, Professor Emeritus, Orange Coast College, Costa
Mesa, CA, and founding president of the Committee for the Restoration of
Democracy in Burma

Twenty-First Century Books
A division of Lerner Publishing Group, Inc.
241 First Avenue North
Minneapolis, MN 55401 U.S.A.

Website address: www.lernerbooks.com

Library of Congress Cataloging-in-Publication Data

Zahler, Diane.
    Than Shwe's Burma / by Diane Zahler.
       p.   cm. – (Dictatorships)
    Includes bibliographical references and index.
    ISBN 978–0–8225–9097–2 (lib. bdg. : alk. paper)
       1. Burma–History–1948—Juvenile literature. 2. Than Shwe–Juvenile
literature. I. Title.
    DS530.65.Z35 2010
    959.105'3–dc22   2008050097

Manufactured in the United States of America
1 2 3 4 5 6 – DP – 15 14 13 12 11 10

CONTENTS

THE MONKS'

BURMA IS A STUNNINGLY BEAUTIFUL COUNTRY in Southeast Asia, bordering Thailand and Laos to the east, China to the north, India and Bangladesh to the northwest, and the Indian Ocean to the west and south. To the outside observer, Burma appears as a land of gray mists, green rice fields, ornate Buddhist temples, jungles, and steep mountains. But outside observers, especially those from the West, can rarely view its wonders up close. Burma's government is a military junta (governing council), which has been run since 1992 by Senior General Than Shwe. Observers have described Than Shwe as uneducated, "sullen," and "brutal." His goal has been to wrap his country in a veil of secrecy, allowing in few reporters or diplomats and strictly controlling the flow of information to and from the rest of the world. And for many years, he was successful. Myanmar, as the government has renamed the country, was rarely in the news—until the summer of 2007.

REBELLION

On August 15, 2007, the government stopped subsidizing (supporting) the price of fuel, reportedly planning to use the extra funds to raise the salaries of government and military officials. Overnight, fuel prices rose by 100 to 500 percent. It was as if a gallon (7.6 liters) of gas, for which we might pay two dollars, suddenly cost eight dollars. Immediately, the cost of public transportation skyrocketed, and the price of food quickly followed. People were unable to feed their families, travel to their jobs, or heat their homes. And to the government's surprise, the people of Burma rose up in protest. They were rebelling not just against the price of fuel but against generations of oppression. The British ambassador to Burma tried to explain the situation to uncaring Burmese government officials, saying, "You need to look very carefully at the underlying political and economic

NAME CHANGE

One of Than Shwe's first actions on ascending to power was to change the name of the country officially to Myanmar, which is the written form of the nation's name in the Burmese language. The term *Burma* is closer to the spoken form of the name. The British called the country Burma when they ruled the land as a British colony. The junta appears to have chosen to use the name Myanmar partly in reaction to the Western use of Burma and partly because they felt the pronunciation of Myanmar was closer to the historical name of the country. However, many Burmese feel that using the name Myanmar shows sympathy with the regime. They prefer the name Burma, despite its association with the colonial past. For the same reason, the governments of the United States and the United Kingdom call the nation Burma. The United Nations (UN), which allows its members to choose what they are called, uses Myanmar, as do France and Japan. The Burmese government also changed other place-names. The capital city of Rangoon, for example, became Yangon, while the Irrawaddy River was renamed the Ayeyarwady.

hardships. The government must also understand what this is about—not fuel prices, but decades of dissatisfaction."

The protests were led by thousands of Buddhist monks, who are revered throughout the country as moral and spiritual leaders. Dressed in traditional maroon robes, they led marches through the streets of Burma's cities and towns. As they marched, thousands of people spilled from their homes to join them. Together, they chanted prayers, including the Metta Sutta, the Buddha's words on loving-kindness.

This is the way of those who are skilled and peaceful, who seek the good and follow the path:

May they be able and upright, straightforward, of gentle speech and not proud.

May they be content and easy wherever they are.

May they be unburdened, with their senses calm.

May they be wise and not arrogant.

May they live without desire for the possessions of others.

May they do no harm to any living being.

The government stayed quiet, perhaps hoping that the protesters would tire of marching and go home, but the demonstrations grew larger. By the end of September, the protesters numbered in the tens of thousands and the junta lost patience. On September

BUDDHIST MONKS MARCH THROUGH THE BURMESE CITY OF RANGOON IN
September 2007 in a protest against government oppression.

INJURED JAPANESE REPORTER KENJI NAGAI PHOTOGRAPHS BURMESE soldiers as they beat protesters in Rangoon on September 27, 2007. Nagai, who was shot when the soldiers tried to disperse the crowd, later died of his wounds.

26, Than Shwe ordered the army to begin using tear gas and clubs against the protesters. Soldiers fired machine guns into the air to frighten the demonstrators and beat monks and civilians alike. They arrested hundreds of monks and killed at least two. Some estimates put the death toll far higher. The army sealed off the monasteries, and no monks were allowed to leave or return.

Suddenly, the eyes of the world were on Burma. With some access to the Internet possible even in this isolated nation, it was no longer easy for the junta to control completely the information coming out of Burma. Hundreds of websites featured pictures of soldiers beating holy men. People everywhere, stunned by the use of violence against the peaceful monks, were swiftly becoming aware of what was happening inside Burma. And the name of Burma's dictator, Than Shwe, was on the lips of newscasters, government leaders, diplomats, and ordinary citizens around the globe.

CHAPTER 1

BURMA

BURMA IS DIVERSE IN ITS LANDFORMS AND CLIMATE. The Northern Mountains, which are part of the Himalayas, lie in the north and west. The highest peak in Southeast Asia is found there—Mount Hkakabo Razi, at 19,295 feet (5,882 meters) high. In the central region, there are low mountains and rich river valleys. Some of the country's major cities are in the central region, including Mandalay. The Shan Plateau is a high tableland bordering China, Laos, and Thailand. The coastal areas along the Bay of Bengal (part of the Indian Ocean) in the south and southwest include the Irrawaddy River delta, where the 1,250-mile-long (2,012-kilometer) Irrawaddy River empties into the bay. Much of the country's rice—a staple crop—grows there. Burma also includes islands in the Bay of Bengal, most of which are uninhabited.

The southern Tenasserim Coast, bordering Thailand, has the largest remaining rain forest in Southeast Asia. There the trees remain green

AND ITS KINGS

VILLAGERS STEER A BOAT DOWN the Irrawaddy River in central Burma. The river is important for transportation as well as farming.

all year, and rain falls nearly every day. Burma also has temperate forests in the northern mountainous areas, where trees lose their leaves every year. The country's weather varies with the region. In the south, the climate is tropical, with year-round heat and humidity. Temperatures can rise to 113°F (45°C). In the north, the temperature can dip below freezing and often snow covers the highest peaks. Despite this wide range of temperature zones, there are three main seasons throughout the country. The monsoon season from mid-May to October is hot and very wet in the south. Monsoons bring drenching rains and winds. From October to mid-February is called the dry season, with winds but little rain, and temperatures are relatively cool. Mid-February to mid-May is the intermonsoon season, when the weather is hot and dry.

The south gets up to 200 inches (508 centimeters) of rain a year. The central plain gets only about 20 to 40 inches (51 to 102 cm) a year.

ETHNIC GROUPS OF BURMA

There are 48 million people living in Burma. This population contains eight major ethnic groups, with 135 subgroups among them. Of the eight, the largest percentage of the population is Bamar, or Burman (68 percent, or about 30 million people). The Bamar came to Burma from the eastern Himalayas more than twelve hundred years ago and settled in the Irrawaddy Valley. They speak a language that is related both to Tibetan and to Chinese. Most of the Bamar are Buddhists.

The next-largest group is the Shan, who originally came from China. They live mostly in the Shan State, though some live in other regions of Burma and also in China and Thailand. Between 9 and 15 percent of the population is Shan. They speak the Shan language, and most also speak Burmese. The Shan generally practice Buddhism, though many are also animists, believing that spirits inhabit natural objects. The Shan farm rice, fruit, vegetables, and soybeans. Some are also involved in mining and logging.

LANGUAGES OF BURMA

A study of the number of languages spoken in Burma begun in the 1920s was abandoned when it found more than 240 different languages. Officially, there are 108 languages spoken in Burma and an extinct language (Pali). The most common language, Burmese, is a tonal language, with high, low, and creaky tones. A tonal language uses voice tone to establish the meaning of words. (English is a stress language, where the emphasis on syllables helps establish meaning.) Thus, a word in Burmese can have many different meanings when it is said with a different tone of voice.

The Karen, or Kayin, about 6 percent of the population, came to Burma from Tibet. Most live in the eastern region of the country in Karen State, bordering Thailand. The majority are Buddhist, though a number of them practice animism. Some Karen are Christian, converted to Christianity in the nineteenth century by U.S. missionaries. Their principal livelihood is agriculture.

The Arakanese, or Rakhine, live in Rakhine State and make up about 4 percent of the population. They are Buddhists and claim to be among the earliest followers of the Buddha. Their culture is strongly influenced by nearby India. They farm mostly rice.

The Mon live in Mon State and along the Thai border. They were among the earliest dwellers in Southeast Asia and helped to spread Buddhism through Burma and Thailand. They came to Burma before

1500 B.C. and were an ethnic majority throughout much of the area until the fifteenth century A.D. In modern times, they comprise about 4 percent of the population. Most make their living in agriculture.

The Karenni, or Kayah, came from Mongolia in the eighth century B.C. and live mostly in the Karenni State on the border of Thailand and Burma. Their name means "Red Karen." They have this nickname because they are a subtribe of the Karen people and often dress in red. Comprising less than 5 percent of the population, most Karenni are Christians. The rest practice Buddhism or animism.

The Kachin people live in the northernmost part of Burma, bordering China. The majority of Kachin are Christian, converted from animism by U.S. missionaries (religious teachers). They farm rice, vegetables, tobacco, and corn. They make up about 3 percent of the population, as do the Chin, who live in Chin State, bordering Bangladesh and India. The Chin came to Burma from China. About 70 percent of the five hundred thousand Chin in Burma are Christians.

In addition to these major ethnic groups, the Rohingya live in Rakhine State and are Muslims (followers of Islam). The Rohingya farm and eat mostly rice. The Wa, who live in the Shan State and are mostly animists, farm rice, but the crop in their hilly country is not sufficient to support them. Many grow opium poppies and are involved in the production of the drug heroin.

BURMA'S ANCIENT HISTORY

The valley of the Irrawaddy River has been home to a series of civilizations over several thousand years. Human settlements appeared about eleven thousand years ago, and more than three thousand years ago, the people of the valley, the Mon, were already making bronze weapons, growing rice, and raising animals for food. The farmers learned to use the waters of the Irrawaddy to irrigate their fields. Their agricultural way of life expanded. By the fourth century B.C., villages, towns, and then cities developed. Each city was controlled by its own government.

Trade closely linked the Mon city-states of Burma with India. The Irrawaddy was easily navigable, and it emptied into the Bay of Bengal, which also borders India. In the third century B.C., Emperor Asoka of India converted to Buddhism. This religion had begun in the Ganges River valley in India in the sixth century B.C. and slowly spread. Many people in nearby Burma followed the emperor's lead. A Chinese traveler described the people of the valley at that time, saying, "It is their custom to love life and hate killing. . . . They do not wear silk because, they say, it comes from silk worms and involves injury to life." This peaceful society was centered in the city-state of Prome (Pyay, or Pye, to the Burmese), which was walled with green bricks that enclosed beautiful buildings. Prome lasted for nearly a thousand years. Beyond Prome, however, Burma was

EMPEROR ASOKA, SHOWN IN THIS drawing from the 1700s, sent Buddhist missionaries to the lands later known as Burma.

changing. In the first century A.D., the Pyu people moved into the northern part of Burma from the valleys of the Himalayas. At the same time, the Shan settled in the east of the country.

BUDDHISM IN BURMA

In the twenty-first century, about 300 million people around the world are Buddhists. There are two main types of Buddhism. Both sprang from the life and teachings of Siddhartha Gautama, called the Buddha (Enlightened One), who lived about twenty-five hundred years ago. Theravada Buddhism, which is practiced in Burma, Thailand, Sri Lanka, Cambodia, and Laos, is based on what are called the Four Noble Truths. These are that humans feel suffering, the cause of suffering is craving, individuals must try to relinquish craving, and individuals must follow the Noble Eightfold Path to relinquish craving.

The Noble Eightfold Path focuses on what people must do to act and meditate rightfully. Individuals try to practice the Four Cardinal Virtues, which are loving-kindness, compassion, joy, and acceptance. Practitioners of Buddhism attempt to achieve nirvana, or perfect bliss, which frees a person from the cycle of birth, aging, death, and rebirth. Theravada Buddhism focuses on meditation— a mental practice—to free the mind from suffering and develop compassion for all. Buddhism divides the population into monks and nuns and laypeople. Each monk or nun takes a vow of poverty and receives food through daily begging. A monk is not permitted to ask for food but will simply stand outside a home with eyes cast down. The laypeople inside then offer the monk food, which allows donors to gain merit through their generosity.

THERAVADA BUDDHISM

In Burma, Theravada monks and nuns follow these ten precepts, or guides, of living:

1. Refrain from murder
2. Refrain from stealing
3. Refrain from sexual misconduct
4. Refrain from lying
5. Refrain from alcohol
6. Refrain from gluttony, or eating after noon
7. Refrain from participating in or watching entertainments
8. Refrain from adorning the body
9. Refrain from the use of high or comfortable beds
10. Refrain from using money

All Buddhists are expected to follow the first five precepts, and novices—or those who are studying in monasteries and considering becoming monks—follow all but the last. When monks are ordained, they must follow all ten, along with 227 *vinayas*, or rules. Nuns (women who pledge their lives to Buddhism) have 311 vinayas to follow.

From Buddhism's earliest days in Burma, the monks' compassion and devotion to the people made them a vital part of Burmese society. When kings embraced Buddhism, their reigns were often more peaceful. Many Burmese kings devoted themselves to building pagodas (temples) dedicated to the Buddha, earning the country the nickname Land of Pagodas. Over the centuries, the monks built their monasteries in village after village and became a vital part of the daily lives of the Burmese. This led to a strong bond between them and the villagers, townspeople, and city dwellers among whom they lived. Nearly 90 percent of modern Burmese are Buddhists.

THE NANZHAO COME CALLING

A group of warrior horsemen inhabited the kingdom of Nanzhao, around Lake Dali in northern Burma, near China. Their civilization was military, and all adult men were required to do army service. In the A.D. 800s, the Nanzhao soldiers began to move into the Irrawaddy Valley. The peaceful city-states fell one by one. After two hundred years of near-constant warfare, the valley belonged to the Nanzhao. Over time the Nanzhao grew less violent under the influence of Buddhism. Many of the valley cities once more became independent.

In the ninth century, a group called the Bamars moved into the area from around the China-Tibet border. They founded the city of Pagan on the banks of the Irrawaddy, upriver from the delta. Pagan grew slowly until the eleventh century, when Anawrahta (also known as Aniruddha), the cousin of the Bamar king, killed the king and claimed the kingdom.

THE CITY OF PAGAN *(ABOVE)* **WAS A RELIGIOUS CENTER AS WELL AS THE SEAT**
of the Bamar government. The Bamars built more than one thousand temples and
shrines in and around the city.

Anawrahta had converted to Buddhism and worked to spread
Buddhism through his land, but his religion did not make him
peaceable. Instead, over the next thirty years, King Anawrahta
reconquered the city-states of the Bamars, which had once more
become independent. He was the first to unify most of present-day
Burma, forming the First Burmese Empire.

Pagan was the capital of Anawrahta's kingdom. It was said to be
a place of wonder, with hundreds of monasteries, libraries, temples,
and colleges decorated with statues, shrines, and mural paintings.
Many of the nobles of Pagan were well educated and spoke several

languages. Anawrahta and his descendants built a network of dams and irrigation systems, greatly increasing the production of rice and other crops. It was a golden age for a united Burma.

THE MONGOLS INVADE

In the 1200s, Genghis Khan had unified the Mongol nation, located south of Siberia in present-day Mongolia. The Mongols were great warriors, and their love of warfare and empire building led them to conquer Russia, China, and Persia (modern Iran). After Genghis Khan's death, his grandson Kublai Khan became emperor and continued to expand his empire's borders, eventually reaching Burma. The Mongols demanded tribute from the city of Pagan, but the Burmese king Narathihapate refused to pay. The khan declared war, sending his well-trained troops—twelve thousand strong—against the Burmese. The Burmese had the advantage, reportedly with an army of sixty thousand soldiers and two thousand elephants. Each elephant carried a wooden tower on its back that held at least a dozen soldiers. The Venetian traveler Marco Polo,

DURING HIS REIGN, KUBLAI KHAN invaded Japan and the lands known in modern times as Vietnam and Java, as well as Burma.

who was living and working at Kublai Khan's court at the time, described what happened when the Mongol soldiers met the elephant troops.

The horses of the Tartars [Mongols] took such fright at the sight of the elephants that they could not be got to face the foe. . . . But their Captain . . . immediately gave orders that every man should dismount and tie his steed to the trees of the forest . . . and that they should take to their bows. . . . Understand that when the elephants felt the smart of those arrows that pelted them like rain, they turned tail and fled, and nothing on earth would have induced them to turn and face the Tartars. So off they sped with such a noise and uproar that you would have trowed [thought] the world was coming to an end!

He went on to describe the battle itself.

Right fiercely did the two hosts rush together, and deadly were the blows exchanged. The king's troops were far more in number than the Tartars, but they were not of such mettle, nor so inured to war. . . . Great was the medley, and dire and parlous [dangerous] was the fight that was fought on both sides; but the Tartars had the best of it.

The Burmese king fled after this battle, and shortly afterward, he was killed by his own son, who soon lost the kingdom to the Mongols. The golden age of Pagan was over. Burma never formally became part of the Mongol Empire, though it was for a short time governed by the faraway court of the emperor. Then the Mongols retreated, and small kingdoms sprang up once again. For the next three hundred years, the Burmese lived again in city-states rather than a single, unified kingdom.

THE RULE OF BAYINNAUNG

In the 1500s, the most powerful city in Burma had become Pegu, near the coast of the Bay of Bengal. Inhabited by the Mon people, Pegu traded with Indians, Greeks, Arabs, and Venetians. It was a beautiful city with educated people who practiced Buddhism.

In a kingdom to the north of Pegu called Taungoo, a general named Bayinnaung plotted with his king to conquer Pegu and the other city-states of Burma and unite the land once more into a single kingdom. At this time, Portugal had become a world power, with colonies on several continents. The Portuguese explorer Vasco da Gama had located a commercial sea route to India, bringing the Portuguese to the area. Fighting alongside hired Portuguese soldiers, Bayinnaung brought down Pegu, proclaimed himself king, and then headed north. He and his troops sailed up the Irrawaddy in wooden warships shaped like elephants and crocodiles. The battles between Bayinnaung's troops and the various groups they encountered continued for years. Finally, Bayinnaung subdued the people of the valley and hills. Then he turned to Siam (present-day Thailand). The Siamese surrendered quickly to this warrior-king, and Bayinnaung returned to Pegu with the king of Siam as his hostage.

A Venetian named Gaspero Balbi traveled to Pegu during the reign of King Bayinnaung, and wrote a description of the city.

There are two Cities of Pegu, the old and the new; in the former Strangers and Merchants inhabit, who are many, and [own] . . . great store of merchandise, in this also is the King's Nobles, and Gentlemen, and other people. The new is not very large, it was built by the father of the present King, on a sudden, in a very neat fashion and with wonderfull strength: The old is very ancient and reasonable great, with many houses made of great caves, and many Magasins [stores] of brick to keep wares in.

The description of the mingling of old and new showed clearly the importance of merchants and their trade and reflected the beginnings of the European influence in Burma.

King Bayinnaung's empire, known by historians as the Second Burmese Empire, held together for almost two hundred years. India pressed against it to the west, and China attacked periodically from the north. But Bayinnaung—as much a myth as a man—had created a strong kingdom. It wasn't until the powers of Europe became involved that Bayinnaung's Burma began to crumble.

THE FRENCH AND BRITISH

By the 1740s, the descendants of Bayinnaung had become weak and ineffectual. The government taxed the people heavily, and finally, they rebelled at Pegu. Led by a nobleman named Binnya Dala, who declared himself king, the revolt spread northward. There it ran into the forces of Aung Zeyya, a Bamar village chief who claimed to be a descendant of a fifteenth-century king and refused to swear loyalty to Binnya Dala. Aung Zeyya quickly organized an army of like-minded villagers.

About this time, the French and British were fighting the Seven Years' War (1756–1763) in Europe. This was a conflict for control of colonies around the world. India was held partly by the French and partly by the British. Both nations wanted supremacy in neighboring Burma. The French befriended Binnya Dala, but Aung Zeyya, who became known as Alaungpaya, or "the future Buddha," was winning every battle. Alaungpaya wanted an alliance with the British and sent a letter to that effect to King George II of Great Britain. He wrote:

> The King [Alaungpaya, speaking of himself], Despotick, of great Merit, of great Power . . . Sovereign of the Kingdom of the Burmars, the Kingdom of Siam and Hughen and the Kingdom of Cassey; Lord of the Mines of Rubies, Gold, Silver, Copper, Iron, and Amber, Lord of the White Elephant, Red Elephant, and Spotted Elephant, Lord of the Vital Golden Lance . . . Salutes the King of England.

King George never replied. Stung, Alaungpaya redoubled his efforts against the French and Binnya Dala, determined to win on his own. He retook Pegu, entering the city on an elephant as his soldiers killed men, women, and children indiscriminately.

King Alaungpaya set up his court at Ava, farther up the Irrawaddy. Over the years, known as the time of the Third Burmese Empire, Alaungpaya and his descendants repelled attacks from China and strengthened their hold on Siam. In an attempt to increase his empire, the Burmese king sent troops into Assam, in present-day India. He won a decisive battle there, and Assam became a Burmese province.

THE BRITISH EAST INDIA COMPANY

The East India Company was a British business created in 1600 under Queen Elizabeth I to develop trade with eastern Asia and India. Before long, the company was heavily involved in politics. It had its own military arm, which helped it to conquer and control the Indian city-states.

With the Seven Years' War ended, the British, represented by the British East India Company, held most of the rest of India. By 1824 the East India Company had begun to consider the Burmese a threat to their hold on India. They may also have been interested in the vast natural resources of Burma, as described by a British surgeon, William Hunter, who traveled through Burma with the East India Company in 1783.

This country is very plentifully supplied with all the necessaries of life. Rice is produced in abundance. The fruits are much the same with those in Bengal; such as pine-apples, water-melons, plantains, &c . . . they have plenty of poultry and game, particularly deer and wild hogs. The forests abound with wild elephants.

The East India Company warned the British king that war with Burma might be necessary, both to protect their interest in India and to gain the precious resources Burma offered. The British made ready.

King Bagyidaw, great-grandson of Alaungpaya, was prepared when the British formally declared war on March 5, 1824. Over the next two years, the army of the British East India Company and the Burmese army fought repeated battles in the First Anglo-Burmese War. A British soldier, Major John James Snodgrass, described an early battle he watched from a British warship.

Having furled sails and beat to quarters, a pause of some minutes ensued, during which not a shot was fired; on our side humanity forbade that we should be the first aggressors upon an almost defenceless town, containing, as we supposed, a large population of unarmed and inoffensive

BRITISH SOLDIERS INVADE A BURMESE STOCKADE AT RANGOON on July 8, 1824, during the First Anglo-Burmese War.

people. . . . The Burmese, on their part, stood for some time inactive at their guns, apparently unwilling to begin the unequal contest; until, urged by the threats and orders of their chiefs, they at length opened their feeble battery on the shipping. The frigate's fire soon silenced every gun on shore; the enemy, unable to withstand her powerful broadside, fled in confusion from their works, and the troops being landed, took possession of a deserted town.

The war cost Great Britain millions of pounds. In all, more than thirty thousand soldiers died, fifteen thousand of them British or Indian. British soldiers also suffered from tropical diseases such as malaria and dysentery. However, their weapons, tactics, and numbers were superior, and by fall of 1826, the Burmese were forced to surrender. The Burmese monarch had to pay a huge tribute and give Britain three provinces. Though the monarchy remained in power, it was greatly weakened. Another war with Great Britain in 1852 resulted in the loss of still more independent territory and left the monarchy in jeopardy. Not only was the Burmese government losing its land to Britain, it was losing the confidence of its people. The British, however, were busy with their outposts in Africa and central Asia, and they turned away from Burma.

THE LAST KINGS

King Mindon took the throne in 1853, deposing his half brother Pagan. A devout Buddhist, Mindon called a meeting of Buddhist leaders to renew and strengthen the Buddhist scriptures. The council lasted for five months, during which the participants examined all the teachings of Buddha in detail and inscribed them on marble slabs that to this day make up the world's largest book. The king was tolerant of other religions as well and built a mosque for the Muslims of Mandalay, the city he made the new capital of his kingdom in 1857. Mindon also tried to modernize the country. Under his rule, he had factories built and brought the telegraph to Burma. Young noblemen were sent to be educated in Europe. The king tried to centralize the government and create a new tax system. However, the people were confused by all these changes. The country was destabilized once again when their confusion turned to rebellion. The government put down the uprising, but rebels assassinated the king's heir, his brother Ka Naung. Reports claim that the reason Mindon survived was that he ran to the man who was supposed to kill him and confronted the assassin. Out of habit, the killer dropped to his knees, whereupon the king leaped onto his back and rode piggyback to safety.

Despite his possibly miraculous escape, the king's position was weakened still further by the rebellion. King Mindon died in 1878 without choosing another heir, and the Council of State appointed nineteen-year-old Prince Thibaw, one of Mindon's lesser sons, to the throne. The king's ministers effectively ran the country, forcing the king to ask them even for money to pay his bills.

Britain turned its attention back to Burma. The viceroy (British governor-general) of India was told to negotiate a trade treaty with Thibaw, but the Burmese government balked. At this time, the government was rife with corruption. Most offices were for sale, and most dealings involved bribes. As the government weakened further, the Shan and Kachin people rebelled in the north. Grasping for power, Burmese officials worked out a secret

KING THIBAW STUDIED IN A BUDDHIST monastery and then ruled in northern Burma before becoming king in 1878.

trade treaty with France, which the British soon discovered. The British feared that the treaty would give the French too much power in Burma. In response, they planned to annex (claim) Upper Burma. Thibaw, furious at these plans, took his revenge by accusing a British trading company, the British Bombay-Burmah Trading Corporation, of cheating the Burmese government out of taxes it owed. He levied an enormous fine on the company. The British government demanded that the Burmese reconsider the fine, and the Burmese refused. This gave the British the excuse they needed to move into Burmese territory in November 1885 and annex Upper Burma. They deposed Thibaw and sent him into exile in India. Less than two weeks later, Burma had become a province of India, run by the British. Its new capital was Rangoon.

THE TWENTIETH

UNDER THE BRITISH, BURMA BECAME a major exporter of rice to the rest of the world. The British brought railroads and steamboats to the country, but the farmers and villagers didn't benefit from these changes because they did not reach into the interior of the country. The British turned many small farms into large rice plantations, as rice was the most lucrative crop, and farmers found themselves displaced by the rice fields. They wandered, jobless and hungry, to the cities. The British did not allow Burmese to work in the civil service, which was staffed mainly by British and Indian workers.

After World War I (1914–1918), independence movements strengthened both in India and in Burma. In the 1920s, students and monks organized strikes to protest excessive taxes and repressive policies in the cities. Students at the University of Rangoon organized a group called the Dobama Asiayone, or We Burmans

BRITISH TROOPS POLICE A BURMESE CITY IN 1930 AFTER PROTESTS
in favor of independence became violent.

Association. Its members called themselves Thakins, which means "masters." The term referred to the British, and the aim of the Thakins was to protest against British rule.

Under pressure from the strikes and protests, in 1937 Britain gave limited autonomy to its various colonial provinces, and Burma Province was separated from India. Burma was still under British rule, but it was allowed to set up a government with a two-house parliament and a prime minister. These changes happened too slowly for many nationalists. Strikes in 1938 led to riots and demonstrations in which protesters were shot and killed. The next year saw Britain's resources turn to fighting World War II (1939–1945). Before the Burmese protests could go further, the Japanese attacked Pearl Harbor in Hawaii on December 7, 1941. Quickly, the Philippines, Hong Kong, Malaya (modern-day Malaysia), and Siam were overrun with Japanese troops. Three weeks later, on December 28, the Japanese bombed Rangoon.

Allied troops from Great Britain, Canada, the United States, Australia, and India converged on Burma, determined to hold off the enemy, but the Japanese fought bitterly to invade and occupy the country. The inhabitants of Rangoon were evacuated to Mandalay, and tens of thousands more fled there ahead of the retreating Allied soldiers. In March the Japanese bombed Mandalay, creating a huge firestorm that leveled most of the city. Within days, the Japanese held the southern half of Burma, and the rest of the country fell quickly.

BURMESE VILLAGERS GATHER BY THE ROADSIDE AS JAPANESE SOLDIERS MARCH toward Rangoon in 1942.

THE RISE OF AUNG SAN

Aung San was a middle-class Burman who discovered an interest in politics before World War II while studying at the University of Rangoon. He joined the student Thakin movement and, with his friend U Nu, led one of the strikes in which students clashed with the British. In 1938 he gave up his studies to enter politics, and in 1940, he traveled to China in search of support for Burma's independence movement. There, the Japanese contacted him. With their help and promise of support, he went back to Rangoon with other rebels and formed a group called the Thirty Comrades. Headed by Aung San and another friend, Ne Win, the Thirty Comrades created the Burma Independence Army (BIA). The army followed behind the Japanese as they swept through Burma. It gathered support from fellow citizens, who were fed up with decades of British oppression. Those Burmese who opposed the BIA were routinely slaughtered.

In 1943 Japan granted formal independence to Burma. The man who had been prime minister before the war, Dr. Ba Maw, became the country's leader. Aung San was his second in command and head of the army. Though Ba Maw was determined to lead Burma as its dictator, in truth the Japanese controlled the country.

In 1944 the Allies attacked the Japanese front line in Burma. For three months, the battle raged, leaving eighty thousand Japanese and seventeen thousand Allied troops dead. The Japanese retreated, and the Allies followed them across the Irrawaddy into Mandalay and then to Rangoon. Ba Maw fled to Japan. Aung San and Ne Win decided, however, that their allegiance was to Burma alone. They had come to distrust Japan's plans for their country, even if the Japanese won the war—which was looking increasingly unlikely.

They formed a resistance movement called the Anti-Facist People's Freedom League (AFPFL) and renamed their army the Burma Defense Army. Switching allegiance in the global conflict, Aung San contacted Admiral Louis Mountbatten, the supreme commander of Allied forces in Southeast Asia. He offered the Allies the services of his army. When the Allied forces moved into Rangoon in 1945, the Burma Defense Army met them as liberators. The Japanese had given up Burma. Aung San and his group had changed sides at exactly the right moment.

The Allies arrested Ba Maw. He ended up after the war in an Allied prison in U.S.-controlled Japan, because of his support of the Japanese and his earlier attempts to keep Burma from working with the Allies in the war effort.

BURMESE NAMES

Burmese do not have family names. Names are usually either one, two, or three syllables and are often chosen in consultation with astrologers. To a Burmese, a name can have a strong effect on a person's life. People's names often start with the first letter of the day of the week they were born. Burmese can change their names and may do so to change their fates. The prefix "U" is a polite form of address meaning "Uncle." "Daw" is the polite form of address for women.

AFTER THE WAR

When Japan surrendered in 1945, Britain attempted to reinstate its rule over Burma. In response, Aung San demanded free elections and raised an army from his old followers and the younger generation, who had seen little but war in their lifetime. They backed Aung San's demands for independence. By 1947 Great Britain had granted India independence. India had its own government and made it clear that it would not help the British in Burma.

GENERAL AUNG SAN SAT FOR THIS
portrait in 1946. He had raised an army
to protest British rule of Burma.

At first, the British wanted to try Aung San as a traitor, based on his earlier alliance with the Japanese. Admiral Mountbatten, however, in charge of Burma's transition from wartime government to civilian government, had not forgotten Aung San's help near the war's end. He sent a representative, Sir Hubert Rance, to head Burma's postwar government. Rance placed Aung San in his administration, and the British government invited Aung San to London. There, he and the British worked out a deal. The temporary government would arrange elections, and then the elected parliament would run Burma.

In April 1947, elections went forward. Aung San's political party, the Anti-Fascist People's Freedom League, won the vast majority of seats in the new parliament. Burma officially withdrew from the British Commonwealth, the association of countries that once had been British possessions. On July 19, however, before independence could be formally declared, a jeep carrying men in soldiers' uniforms drove up to the government offices in Rangoon. The men entered the room where the provisional government was meeting and opened fire, shooting Aung San and six other council members. The architect of Burma's independence died in a hail of gunfire before he could see his dream fully realized.

"*The welfare of all people of this country irrespective of race or religion has always been the one purpose that I have set out to fulfill. In fact it is my life's mission. Unfortunately, the country to which you and I belong is not yet free. Unless our nation has the freedom to plan our destiny and life in accordance with our head's vision and heart's desire, it will not be possible to promote the welfare of our people to the extent that we wish to do.*"

—Aung San, in a speech to the Anglo-Burman Council, 1946

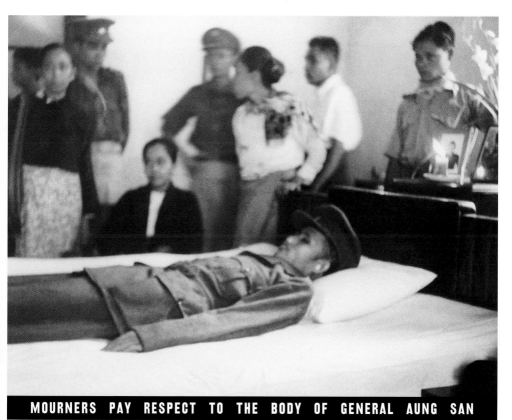

MOURNERS PAY RESPECT TO THE BODY OF GENERAL AUNG SAN at his home following his assassination in 1947. His widow, Khin Kyi, sits nearby between security guards.

The mystery of Aung San's death has never been solved. There are still rumors of a conspiracy involving the British, but the new Burmese government blamed U Saw, who had been prime minister of Burma from 1940 to 1942. He had run for prime minister again in the elections just past and lost. He was tried, hanged, and buried in an unmarked grave.

In January 1948, the last of the British troops in Burma and their commander boarded a ship and sailed away, leaving the country independent at last. But though independent, Burma was not at peace.

NE WIN AND U NU

The first prime minister of an independent Burma was U Nu, one of the few council members who had survived the bloodbath that killed Aung San. He immediately faced uprisings by a group of Communists (believers in a government that controls factories and farms and other means of production) who claimed that Aung San and his followers had been working for the British. The Communists quickly took over the towns and cities along the Irrawaddy. Ne Win, heading an army of Karens and other ethnic groups, fought back, holding off the Communist advances. Ne Win's army quickly grew in number and power and subdued the rebels. By 1950 the country was nearly at peace. U Nu, beloved by many for his mild manner

PRIME MINISTER U NU *(LEFT)* WORKED WITH GENERAL NE WIN *(RIGHT)* to maintain peace between ethnic and political groups after Burma became an independent nation in the 1940s.

and devotion to Buddhism, was firmly in power. He appointed U Thant, a friend from college days, to be press director and secretary of the Ministry of Information.

In 1949 Communists were officially in control of mainland China, with Mao Zedong as the government's leader. The army of the Chinese Nationalists, who opposed the Communists, decided to use Burma as a base for its resistance. They recruited soldiers from the Burmese population and took over a part of northeastern Burma. They trained Burmese guerrilla fighters (not part of an official military) to fight in China. The Nationalist army presence weakened the Burmese government and angered the three hundred thousand Burmese Communists who supported the Communist government in China. The Burmese army fought to remove the guerrillas from Burmese soil. In response, the guerrillas joined forces with rebel ethnic groups who needed little excuse to rise up against the government.

The Burmese government called on the United Nations to ask the Chinese Nationalists to withdraw, but the UN's reaction was halfhearted. The UN appointed a military commission to work with the Nationalists on their withdrawal from Burma, but little action actually took place. Some historians and the Burmese government believe that the United States, fearful that the Communist Chinese would expand their reach throughout Southeast Asia, were secretly supporting the Nationalists. This angered the Burmese government, which stopped accepting aid from the United States and all other foreign countries. In addition, Burmese officials decided they had to strengthen the army to guard against foreign threats from the West. It was the beginning of the country's turn away from the rest of the world.

General Ne Win took charge of the army, and by the late 1950s, the Burmese were able to push out the Chinese Nationalists. Over the next few years, the army broadened its reach. It took over a shipping company, then a bank, and then many import-export businesses. It started its own newspaper. U Nu and U Thant, who had become Burma's UN representative, traveled around the world, presenting a face of friendly neutrality to governments abroad. Meanwhile, Ne Win consolidated power at home.

In 1958 the uneasy peace presided over by U Nu fell apart completely. Soldiers under the direction of General Ne Win took over the government offices. The general told U Nu that he would have to step down. U Nu had no choice but to agree. On September 26, he gave a radio address explaining that he had invited Ne Win to take charge of the government.

Under Ne Win's military regime, the country ran smoothly. Life improved for many Burmese. Prices were stable. The streets were clean. The Communist insurgents were under control. Ne Win had promised the country that he would hold elections in 1960, and he kept his word. Much to the general's shock, though, the people ignored the positive effects of his government. They put U Nu back in power. Ne Win backed away, but he and his army stood in the wings, waiting for another opportunity.

THE MILITARY STATE OF BURMA

During the two years that followed U Nu's election, Ne Win's attitude and aims changed drastically. Maybe the taste of power he had in 1958 to 1960 made him long for more. Maybe he was angered that U Nu's government was about to nationalize, or take over, the companies that the army controlled, putting a stop to the huge profits Ne Win was earning.

U Nu's passage of a constitutional amendment making Buddhism the state religion had angered the Christian minority, destabilizing the country and making U Nu's position shaky. Ne Win saw his opportunity. In March 1962, Ne Win's army marched into Rangoon and took over the government once again, this time arresting U Nu and the other ministers. Ne Win disbanded parliament, suspended the constitution, and created a revolutionary council. In consolidating

A CONVOY OF NE WIN'S TROOPS ARRIVES IN RANGOON IN MARCH 1962.

The soldiers blocked entrances to government offices and arrested ministers.

power, he made himself president, defense minister, and finance minister all in one. The army took over local governments and courts, and silenced the press. Westerners, both individuals and groups, were forced to leave the country. Ne Win closed nightclubs, banned dancing and horse racing, and closed the airports to foreign air service.

Ne Win named his political party the Burma Socialist Program Party (BSPP), but the government was really a military dictatorship. The BSPP was the only legal political party allowed in the country. Its Socialist aim was to nationalize the economy, putting the land and businesses of Burma under government control. The party published a long description of its philosophy, called the Burmese Way to Socialism. It stated that

> The Revolutionary Council of the Union of Burma does not believe that man will be set free from social evils as long as pernicious economic systems exist in which man exploits man and lives on the fat of such appropriation. The Council believes it to be possible only when exploitation of man by man is brought to an end and a socialist economy based on justice is established; only then can all people, irrespective of race or religion, be emancipated from all social evils and set free from anxieties over food, clothing and shelter, and from inability to resist evil, for an empty stomach is not conducive to wholesome morality, as the Burmese saying goes.

Nationalization did not work out as Ne Win had planned, however. There were few qualified managers in the party to run the nationalized businesses. Over the next decade, production levels fell and unemployment skyrocketed. Before long, forgetting that "an empty stomach is not conducive to wholesome morality," the government had to ration food. Ne Win had to back off from his desire for total power. He promised the country a new constitution, which was written and ratified in 1973. Burma held elections for the People's Assembly and local governments, and Ne Win was elected president. After the elections, the economy improved to some extent. Ne Win continued his more liberal policies, allowing some foreign aid into the country and offering amnesty (legal pardon) to political opponents who came forward. Among the few who took advantage of this offer was U Nu, who had been living in exile in India for ten years. On his return, he entered a Buddhist monastery.

THE ECCENTRIC GENERAL

Ne Win was known for his eccentricities and superstition. He was said to bathe in dolphin blood and believed in spells and rituals. He withdrew most of the country's money supply and established new money notes in Burma, with coins and bills in denominations of 45 and 90 because he believed in the magical properties of the number 9. One rumor states that he did this because an astrologer told him that if he did, he would live to be ninety. In fact, he died at ninety-one.

8-8-88

In the 1980s, Ne Win replaced the Burmese banknotes with 15-, 35-, 45-, and 90-kyat notes, entirely due, apparently, to his superstitious belief in the power of the numbers. He did not compensate people for the value of their old banknotes. Many people lost their savings and their jobs. As food became scarce, students in the capital city of Rangoon began to stage demonstrations against the government. In March a fight broke out in a Rangoon tea shop. The police arrested dozens, including many students, but one student, who was the son of a government official, was released. This angered the other students still more. A few days later, another demonstration ended in violence. Soldiers and riot police beat several students to death, and others drowned in Rangoon's Inya Lake in the general mayhem. After police arrested demonstrators, more than thirty students suffocated in a police van as they were driven to prison. Anger and fear grew. Buddhist monks joined in the protests. More than ten thousand people swelled the ranks of the demonstrators. The government closed down the universities, but when they reopened in June, the students marched again. A terrible battle left more than one hundred dead, both students and police.

Ne Win, urged by the army, made a speech in which he announced that he was stepping down. He claimed that the people could elect a parliament and create a new constitution. His words were not enough to stop the marches and rallies. Either the populace did not believe him or did not think events were moving quickly enough. At 8:08 A.M. on August 8, what many claim is a favorable time and day in the Buddhist belief system, workers began to walk off their jobs and march toward the center of the city.

POLICEMEN AND GOVERNMENT WORKERS LEFT THEIR JOBS TO JOIN
protests in Rangoon in August 1988. As protests grew, the government ordered
workers to return to their posts.

At first the army was quiet. After three hours, though, the government reacted. It cut off electricity across Rangoon, and soldiers lined up with their weapons drawn. As the protesters sang the national anthem, the soldiers opened fire on the unarmed marchers.

The government imposed martial law (restrictions on citizens' activities, including curfews) on the country, but the bloodshed continued. Troops fired on doctors and nurses who tended the wounded and dying. High school and college students died in the streets, along with maroon-clad monks. The exact number of deaths is unknown. Estimates range from three to ten thousand. Thousands more were thrown into prison, and many of them were tortured by military officials.

The protests went on, and on August 12, Ne Win's BSPP named Dr. Maung Maung as head of state. He lifted martial law, but peace did not return to the country. People looted stores, rioted in the streets, and burned their BSPP membership cards. Students called for a general strike. The government inexplicably opened the prisons, and criminals ranged free in the cities. By September the country was in an uproar. On September 15, the army stepped in again, attacking and killing hundreds, including monks. Students fled into the countryside and across the borders. The uprising was over.

SOLDIERS DRIVE PRO-DEMOCRACY PROTESTERS OUT OF THE STREETS OF Rangoon during the 1988 protests.

"In order to bring a timely halt to the deteriorating conditions on all sides all over the country and in the interest of the people, the defense forces have assumed all power in the state with effect from today."

—Burmese government radio announcement on September 18, 1988

As a result of 8-8-88, as the rebellion came to be known, the army threw out the premise of the Burma Socialist Program Party. They created a junta, which called itself the State Law and Order Restoration Council, or SLORC. Though it was widely assumed that Ne Win retained at least some of his power, working from behind the scenes, a group of generals vied to control the junta and, through it, the country. One of these military men was General Than Shwe.

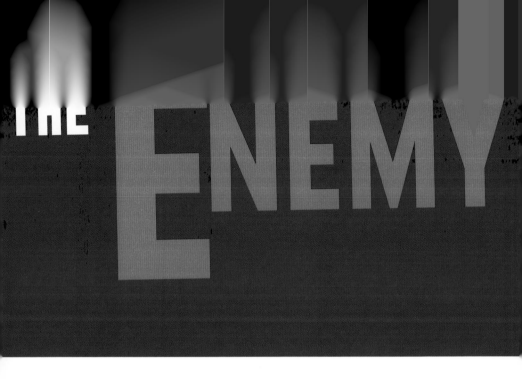

THE ENEMY

THERE IS ONE VOICE OF OPPOSITION in Burma that has rung out against the SLORC since its earliest days. Aung San Suu Kyi, the daughter of nationalist hero Aung San, has been under house arrest off and on since 1989. She is the voice of the opposition political party, the winner of a Nobel Peace Prize, the hope of the Burmese people—and the government's greatest threat. To understand the nature of Burma's dictatorship, one needs to consider the opposition that it has created.

AUNG SAN SUU KYI

Aung San Suu Kyi, whose name means "Strange Collection of Bright Victories," was born in 1945 to Aung San and his wife, Khin Kyi. Aung

AUNG SAN STANDS WITH HIS WIFE, KHIN KYI, AND AUNG SAN SUU KYI
in front of their home in Rangoon in the 1940s.

San Suu Kyi never really knew her father, who was murdered when she was only two years old. As she grew up, though, her father's supporters continually told her stories of his courage and greatness. Her mother, respected as the widow of the country's founder, became an ambassador to India under U Nu. When General Ne Win came to power, however, Khin Kyi retired from political life.

Aung San Suu Kyi was educated in a bilingual Methodist school in Rangoon and completed her secondary schooling in India, where she moved when her mother became ambassador. She entered college in India to study political science. After two years, she won a place at Saint Hugh's College, Oxford University, in England. At Oxford she studied politics, philosophy, and economics. There, she met Michael Aris, an educated, cultured young man who had lived all over the world. A romance blossomed between them, but Aung San Suu Kyi, as the daughter of Aung San, was hesitant to marry a non-Burmese. She went to the United States as a graduate student at New York University, while Aris took a post as tutor to the royal family of Bhutan, a small country in the mountains north of India.

In New York in the late 1960s, Aung San Suu Kyi worked as an assistant secretary for a budget committee of the UN. She spent time with U Thant, a compatriot of her father, and U Nu. U Thant had been elected secretary-general of the United Nations. In U Thant's company, she learned about world politics and the workings of the UN, which would serve her well in later life.

She and Michael Aris found they could not stay apart, so Aung San Suu Kyi moved to Bhutan, taking a job in the Bhutan Ministry of Foreign Affairs. In 1970 she and Aris became engaged, and they married in 1972 in England, in both British civil and Buddhist ceremonies.

The couple returned to Bhutan, where Aung San Suu Kyi took a position advising the government on UN affairs. In 1973 she gave birth to a son, Alexander, and the family returned to England in 1974. She had another son, Kim, in 1977. Over the next eleven years, Aung San Suu Kyi wrote a brief biography of her father and then a series of guide books to Burma, Bhutan, and Nepal. She continued her studies in Burmese literature and Burmese history as a visit-

MICHAEL ARIS AND AUNG SAN SUU KYI POSED FOR THIS PICTURE in Burma around 1973, shortly after they were married in England.

ing scholar at Kyoto University in Japan. She was about to begin work toward a Ph.D. in England in March of 1988, when everything changed for her. The phone rang, and she picked it up to learn that her mother in Burma had had a stroke.

BACK IN BURMA

Aung San Suu Kyi returned to Burma in April 1988 to care for her mother. By that time, Ne Win had been in power for twenty-six years. The country was in deep trouble, socially and economically. Students at the University of Rangoon had begun demonstrating against the government the month before, and Ne Win's reprisals had been violent. As Aung San Suu Kyi tended her mother in Rangoon General Hospital, she saw the beaten and wounded students coming in for treatment. She heard their stories of abuse at the hands of the army and police. Gradually she began to understand the dire condition of the country she had been away from for so long.

Aung San Suu Kyi moved her mother home, and her family came from England to join her. Almost immediately she began getting visits from people who had been close to her father. One man, U Tin Oo, had been imprisoned by Ne Win for four years. He and the others were determined to undermine or overthrow the regime. Tensions mounted between the army and the rebels, spearheaded by students and striking workers. Then the massacre of 8-8-88 took place.

After 8-8-88, a group of teachers from the University of Rangoon urged Aung San Suu Kyi to step up and lead the rebellion. She offered to mediate between the rebels and the government but said she was not ready to take on a leadership role. The rebels continued to pressure her to become their leader, and finally, she agreed to speak to demonstrators. On August 26, 1988, she spoke before a huge crowd in front of the gold-encrusted Shwedagon Pagoda in central Rangoon. Estimates of the crowd range from three hundred thousand to one million people. Wearing traditional Burmese clothing, sandals, and a sarong, or *longyi*, over a modest blouse, she asked for reconciliation. She urged calm, deliberation, and unity. The crowd, thrilled at having the daughter of the heroic Aung San before them, roared its approval.

AUNG SAN SUU KYI *(AT MICROPHONE)* **SPEAKS AT THE SHWEDAGON PAGODA IN** Rangoon on August 26, 1988.

Despite Aung San Suu Kyi's call for peace and discipline, protests and violence continued. The army took steps to quell the uprising. It deposed Ne Win and his Burma Socialist Program Party and replaced the president with the military junta. The reign of the State Law and Order Restoration Council had begun.

Michael Aris and the children returned to England when school started, but Aung San Suu Kyi remained in Rangoon with her ailing mother. As the date for the election promised by the SLORC neared, she began working with U Tin Oo to create a new political party, the National League for Democracy (NLD). The SLORC had made such political parties legal, hoping that so many would spring up that no one party would take more seats than its own party, the National

Unity Party (NUP). The NLD was well organized and attracted intellectuals, lawyers, and students. Aung San Suu Kyi, the party's general secretary, began campaigning in October, giving speeches in towns and villages throughout the country. Large crowds greeted her everywhere she went.

In December, Aung San Suu Kyi's mother died. Her funeral procession passed through streets with tens of thousands of mourners lined up in support of Aung San's wife and daughter. The funeral brought to the SLORC's attention the enormous influence Aung San Suu Kyi had on the Burmese people. When she returned to campaigning, soldiers threatened her at one of her stops in the Irrawaddy Delta region. As they aimed their weapons at her, she stood firm. The soldiers did not dare fire. Word of this showdown spread quickly, making the army look powerless and ridiculous.

"I believe that all the people who have assembled here have without exception come with the unshakeable desire to strive for and win a multi-party democratic system. In order to arrive at this objective, all the people should march unitedly in a disciplined manner towards the goal of democracy."

—Aung San Suu Kyi, in a 1988 speech

SOLDIERS FROM THE BURMESE ARMY ARREST A STUDENT AT A
National League for Democracy rally in 1989.

HOUSE ARREST

The government began arresting and imprisoning members of
the NLD, but they did not touch Aung San Suu Kyi. They feared the
public's response. Instead, on July 20, 1989, the army placed her
under house arrest, sealing her off from the rest of the world inside
her home on University Avenue in Rangoon. Soldiers guarded the
house night and day, and the house number was removed so supporters could not find her and rally there.

Soldiers built watchtowers and checkpoints along the road to keep supporters from visiting her.

Through Michael Aris, however, the world quickly found out what had happened. He went to Burma with his sons and was permitted to see his wife, who by this time had begun a hunger strike. She demanded that the regime treat the NLD members in prison with humanity. News of the hunger strike leaked out, and after twelve days, the SLORC gave in to her demands, assuring her that prisoners would not be maltreated.

The SLORC then arrested and imprisoned U Tin Oo, sentencing him to hard labor. They informed Aung San Suu Kyi that she could not run as a candidate in the upcoming elections because she was married to a foreigner. The NLD still had hundreds of other candidates running for the many local, state, and national positions, though, and on May 27, 1990, the Burmese cast their votes. There were a total of 2,300 candidates from 93 different political parties. The NLD won 80 percent of the political seats they ran for—a total of 392 seats. The regime's party, the NUP, won only 10 seats.

It became clear to the SLORC that Aung San Suu Kyi and her party would bring down their regime if she were free. They ignored the election results. They did not permit Aris to visit again. Aung San Suu Kyi's contact with the world was limited to her radio. Aris, along with others his wife had known and befriended around the world, worked hard to keep Aung San Suu Kyi in the public eye.

THE MISSING MEMBERS OF PARLIAMENT

Many of the 392 NLD members of parliament elected in 1990 are no longer visible in Burma's public life. Of these, 13 are in prison, 20 are in exile, and 84 have died. Of the dead, 3 passed away in custody and 2 were assassinated. Many of the members of parliament living in exile have banded together to form the National Coalition Government of the Union of Burma, a government in exile for the Burmese people. Through Internet sites and newspapers, they attempt to keep Burmese at home and abroad informed about what is happening in their country and their goals for the future, should the military government change. Of those still alive, out of prison, and living in Burma, many continue to work with the NLD, in constant danger of harassment or imprisonment.

CHAPTER 4

THAN SHWE

THAN SHWE, THE NEW DICTATOR OF BURMA, was born on February 2, 1933, in Kyaukse, in central Burma. Burma at that time was controlled by Great Britain through its government in India. Unlike most of the men who governed post-colonial Burma, Than Shwe did not go to college. In fact, some reports claim he didn't finish high school. He went to work as a postal clerk instead.

At the age of twenty, Than Shwe joined the army and found his calling. He went to officer training school and rose quickly through the ranks, at one point serving in the psychological warfare division. In 1960 he was promoted to captain. He worked closely with General Ne Win to overthrow U Nu's government in 1962. He was rewarded for his service with promotions and became a colonel in 1978. Ne Win also appointed him as an instructor at the Central Institute of Political Science, an oddity given his lack of education.

IN POWER

GENERAL THAN SHWE ADDRESSES military personnel during celebrations of Armed Forces Day each year.

By 1980 Than Shwe was in charge of the 88th Light Infantry Division of the Burmese army. Then in his mid-forties, he had a wife, Kyaing Kyaing, and three daughters. Reports by the *New Internationalist*, an international magazine that focuses on global issues, and the Associated Press claim that he spent his time at his new post giving gifts to soldiers, playing golf, reading *Time* magazine, and waging "a brutal campaign against ethnic minority rebels." Compared to other high-ranking officers, his lifestyle was restrained. He sent his children to school in an army truck while others used limousines. His colleagues at the time thought of him as honest and obedient. In 1985 he was promoted to brigadier general and given the title of vice chief of staff of the army. A year later, he won another promotion and became a member of the Executive Committee of Ne Win's Burma Socialist Program Party.

After the uprising of 8-8-88 that brought down Ne Win, Than Shwe helped to found the State Law and Order Restoration Council and became one of its cabinet members. The SLORC was headed by General Saw Maung, who proclaimed himself prime minister and imposed martial law throughout the country. Ne Win's military government had been replaced by another military government, but there were some changes. The SLORC quickly moved to reform Burma's failing economy.

They paid special attention to the plight of poverty-stricken workers and peasants, providing food and housing that had grown scarce under Ne Win's failed Socialist program. They also allowed foreign trade and investment for the first time in decades.

After the elections of May 1990, the results of which the government had ignored, the NUP worked to consolidate the government to ensure their total power would continue. However, there was dissension within its

GENERAL SAW MAUNG JOINED the Burmese army in 1949. He headed the junta council and proclaimed himself prime minister in 1988.

ranks. Between 1990 and 1992, several council members "retired" on the grounds of ill health. Outside political analysts took this to mean that they were forced out of office by more powerful council members. In April 1992, Saw Maung stepped down suddenly, also claiming poor health. The new chairman of the council, secretary of defense, and head of state was Than Shwe.

At first, General Than Shwe seemed to be a less restrictive ruler than Saw Maung. He claimed that "the military would not hold onto power for long," and he allowed party secretary Khin Nyunt to arrange Burma's entry into the Association of Southeast Asian Nations (ASEAN), a group established in 1969 to promote economic growth in the area. This opened the country to outside visitors for the first time in many years. The general permitted human rights groups to visit Burma, and he changed the name of the government party from SLORC to the more friendly sounding State Peace and Development Council (SPDC).

THAN SHWE AND AUNG SAN SUU KYI

In 1991 Aung San Suu Kyi, still under house arrest, was awarded the Sakharov Prize for Freedom of Thought by the European Parliament, the legislature of the European Union. And on October 14, 1991, Norway announced that she would be the recipient of the Nobel Peace Prize.

Because she could not leave her house to make an acceptance speech, her older son, Alexander, still a teenager, spoke for her.

ALEXANDER ARIS *(CENTER)* ACCEPTS THE NOBEL PEACE PRIZE ON BEHALF OF HIS mother, Aung San Suu Kyi, in 1991. His brother, Kim Aris *(right)*, stands next to him.

I stand before you here today to accept on behalf of my mother, Aung San Suu Kyi, this greatest of prizes, the Nobel Prize for Peace. . . . I know that she would begin by saying that she accepts the Nobel Prize for Peace not in her own name but in the name of all the people of Burma. She would say that this prize belongs not to her but to all those men, women and children who, even as I speak, continue to sacrifice their wellbeing, their freedom and their lives in pursuit of a democratic Burma. Theirs is the prize and theirs will be the eventual victory in Burma's long struggle for peace, freedom and democracy.

I know that if she were free today my mother would, in thanking you, also ask you to pray that the oppressors and the oppressed should throw down their weapons and join together to build a nation founded on humanity in the spirit of peace.

Aung San Suu Kyi placed the money from the award, $1.3 million, in a special fund to promote Burmese health and education. She has done the same with most of the proceeds from other awards she has won.

At about the same time as the Nobel Peace Prize announcement, Aung San Suu Kyi's book *Freedom from Fear* was published. It is a collection of speeches and essays by and about her, put together by her husband. It includes her short biography of her father and writings on Buddhism, the people and customs of Burma, and political philosophy. Some of the writings were done before her return to Burma. Others she composed while campaigning for the 1990 elections. The Nobel Peace Prize and her book placed Aung San Suu Kyi very much in the public eye and in Than Shwe's line of vision.

"Among the basic freedoms to which men aspire that their lives might be full and uncramped, freedom from fear stands out as both a means and an end. A people who would build a nation in which strong, democratic institutions are firmly established as a guarantee against state-induced power must first learn to liberate their own minds from apathy and fear."

—Aung San Suu Kyi, "Freedom from Fear," speech given July 10, 1990

As Than Shwe briefly relaxed restrictions within Burma, Aris was able to visit his wife, Aung San Suu Kyi. He reported that she spent her time reading, listening to the radio, playing the piano, gardening, sewing, and writing. Many of her articles and speeches were smuggled out of Rangoon and published. Over the next three years, the government gradually loosened its hold on her. They permitted her to attend a relative's funeral, speak with a *New York Times* reporter and U.S. representative Bill Richardson of New Mexico, and meet with Than Shwe, a meeting that had no discernible effect on the government's policies. Nevertheless, on June 10, 1995, the government inexplicably announced that her house arrest was over.

By the following morning, thousands of people had collected outside Aung San Suu Kyi's house. She spoke to them each morning for a week and then on a weekly basis. She began working again with the NLD, and U Tin Oo, released from prison, continued to help her. She gave interviews to newspapers, news magazines, and even

AUNG SAN SUU KYI SPEAKS TO A CROWD FROM THE GATE OF HER HOUSE on the day after her release from house arrest in 1995.

fashion magazines. She met with the U.S. ambassador to the U.N., Madeleine Albright, who afterward condemned the Burmese government for its restrictive policies.

That same year, the SPDC called a constitutional convention, but it banned all but a few NLD members from the process. In protest over the sham, the remaining NLD members walked out. The constitution took fourteen years to create. Critics have called the document, finally completed in September 2007, a "ruse [trick] to consolidate the military's power" under the guise of democratic concessions.

In May 1996, the government arrested thousands of NLD members, and in retaliation, the league threatened to draft its own constitution. The government responded by beginning to harass the people who came to hear Aung San Suu Kyi's weekly speeches. They began to limit her movements as well. They refused entry visas to her husband and sons. And then, in early 1999, she suffered a personal disaster. Michael Aris phoned to tell his wife that he had advanced prostate cancer and was dying.

Aung San Suu Kyi knew that if she left Burma to see her husband, the junta would not let her return. She had to make a choice between visiting her dying husband and abandoning her country. Probably hoping she would choose to go, the government refused to grant Aris a visa to visit his wife, and they cut off his phone calls to her. On March 27, 1999, Aris died, not having seen his wife since 1995. Tributes to him came from around the world—from U.S. president Bill Clinton; from the Tibetan Buddhist leader, the Dalai Lama; and from Kofi Annan, the secretary-general of the UN. Than Shwe allowed Aung San Suu Kyi's sons to visit her briefly as she mourned, but after these short visits, the government denied further entry visas.

Aung San Suu Kyi threw herself into her work with the NLD. She continued to write political speeches and articles and to give

JOURNALISTS AND SUPPORTERS SURROUND AUNG SAN SUU KYI'S CAR
during her May 2000 standoff with police outside Rangoon.

interviews by telephone. As people around the globe read her words and saw her image on videos smuggled out of Burma, the State Peace and Development Council again began to tighten its hold on her. In May 2000, she tried to drive out of Rangoon and the police blocked her car. She stayed inside the vehicle for nine days, refusing to go back. Soldiers returned her forcibly, and again, she tried to leave. Again, she was forced to return. She was once more placed under house arrest.

This time, the incarceration lasted for nineteen months. When Than Shwe again, without explanation, released her in 2002, the government named her a "visitor" to Burma, not a citizen. She began a speaking tour of the country. The government tracked her every movement, sending groups of men to harass and intimidate her. They warned the people to stay away, but as always, the Burmese flocked to hear her speak. Than Shwe and his cohorts grew more and more furious as her trip progressed. Finally, in the town of Depayin, armed men attacked Aung San Suu Kyi's group. Dozens of NLD members were arrested, beaten, or killed. U Tin Oo was dragged from his car and beaten. Aung San Suu Kyi was arrested and thrown into jail.

After the attack, Aung San Suu Kyi was transferred to a military camp outside Rangoon. World leaders, hearing of the violence against her, called for her release. The junta placed her back under house arrest, and after a brief stay in a hospital (the reasons for which are unclear), she returned to her home on University Avenue. U Tin Oo was also put under house arrest.

Aung San Suu Kyi continued to remain in the public eye despite the government's restrictions. While under house arrest, she won many awards, including the Jawaharlal Nehru Award for International Understanding from the Government of India, the Madanjeet Singh Prize for the Promotion of Tolerance and Non-Violence from UNESCO (a United Nations agency), the Pearl S. Buck Woman of the Year Award, the Franklin D. Roosevelt Freedom from Fear Award, and the Presidential Medal of Freedom from the United States. Many universities have given her honorary degrees. She has been the focus of a film and a play, and musicians from U2 to Paul McCartney to Coldplay have dedicated songs to her. The U.S. Congress awarded her the Congressional Gold Medal, the country's highest civilian honor. Each of these honors and awards only served to fuel Than Shwe's growing hatred for and fear of her. Reports stated he would not even allow her name to be spoken in his presence. After the violent crackdown in September 2007, he has allowed her to meet with members of the NLD and representatives from the United Nations, though in May 2008, he extended her house arrest by another year. Regardless of his personal animosity toward her, he has been unable to silence her or keep her from the world's attention.

A NEW CAPITAL

As the furor over the junta's treatment of Aung San Suu Kyi grew, fueled by critical reports from visiting diplomats and rights groups, Than Shwe became increasingly secretive, repressive, and even paranoid. He arrested Prime Minister Khin Nyunt, whom he saw as a challenge to his power, and imprisoned hundreds of Khin Nyunt's supporters. He banned foreign reporters and stopped news from being reported freely within the country. Rumors circulated of torture in military prisons and the displacement and murder of huge numbers of the ethnic minorities within Burma's borders.

In 2005 Than Shwe relocated the capital of Burma, which had been Rangoon, 200 miles (320 km) north to Naypyidaw, a city built expressly for that purpose. Naypyidaw is in the geographical center of Burma, in an area of tropical scrubland. The general's reasons for relocating the capital are unclear. One theory is that he felt the new location would be more secure from a possible naval invasion. Another rumor is that Than Shwe had a vision that told him to build the city. Other theories posit that the junta built Naypyidaw to protect itself from the growing unrest of its people or that Than Shwe wanted to leave his mark on history by creating a new capital, as the Burmese kings of old did. Than Shwe gave government employees two days to move to the new capital, and when they arrived there, they found there was no housing for them. The British *Times*

NEW APARTMENT BUILDINGS HOUSE GOVERNMENT WORKERS IN NAYPYIDAW
in 2007. While Naypyidaw lacks many amenities, it is one of the few Burmese cities with a constant supply of electricity.

Online described the new city, which in 2007 had no public airport, no cell phone service, and could only be reached via a pothole-ridden two-lane road.

> This is Naypyidaw, the "Place of the Kings," the most myste-rious and bizarre capital city in the world. Its broad roads, grandiose public buildings and shopping centres are meant as a model of the advanced Asian city—but many of them stand empty and unused. Unknown millions have been lavished on its construction, in a country where most people live on less than a dollar a day.

THE SULLEN DICTATOR

The words and phrases that reporters, diplomats, and others use to describe Than Shwe are almost all unflattering. They make it clear that over time, both his personality and his actions have become increasingly extreme and often unpredictable. Soon after his rise to power, an Associated Press article called him a "bulldog" and said he was a "hard-liner" and an "adept political manipulator." A retired World Bank executive said of him, "Than Shwe is such an old fox. . . . I don't see him as a compromiser."

> "Than Shwe can be very charming and friendly when he wants to be . . . but they [the members of the junta] don't like intrusiveness. They don't like you asking about things that they consider to be their internal affairs."
>
> –Razali Ismail, UN expert on Burma, 2007

Later in his reign, the *New Internationalist* stated he was "sullen and unresponsive." The British *Guardian* called him "paranoid, insular, and inept," while the *Irrawaddy*, published in Thailand by and for the Burmese, described him as "manic, xenophobic [afraid of outsiders], and superstitious." Reports have Than Shwe regularly consulting a blind astrologist named E Thi. The *Irrawaddy* described a ceremony at a Buddhist temple in 2006 that shows the general's superstitious nature and his belief in the power of the number 9—a belief shared by his predecessor, Ne Win.

> The auspicious [lucky] number nine figures large in the ritual followed by Than Shwe and his retinue [followers]—a gong is struck nine times, after which Than Shwe, accompanied by his wife, drives the last of nine stakes into the ground where the new pagoda, called Uppatasanti, will be built. Then he sprinkles scented water in the center of the site, while eight military leaders take up positions at eight [other] corners of the site and the bejeweled stakes are struck nine times with golden maces [staffs] and anointed with scented water.

THAN SHWE AND HIS WIFE, Kyaing Kyaing, visit a Buddhist shrine in India in 2004.

Than Shwe lives lavishly, in contrast to his modest lifestyle during his early days in the army. He gives jewels and cars to family members while the vast majority of the Burmese people suffer without adequate housing or food. When Than Shwe's daughter married in 2006, the wedding was called the most sumptuous in Burmese history. It was said to cost more than three hundred thousand dollars. A contraband (unauthorized) video of the wedding was released on the Internet. It showed the bride draped in jewels, a golden wedding bed, and the bridal party drinking quantities of expensive champagne. The video sparked outrage among the Burmese who saw it and compared the harsh living conditions of the average Burmese with the spectacle of this wedding.

THAN SHWE'S GOVERNMENT

Than Shwe's official title is chairman of the State Peace and Development Council. Below him is the vice chairman, Maung Aye, and the prime minster, Thein Sein. A government minister is in

THAN SHWE *(LEFT)* **AND MAUNG AYE** *(RIGHT)* **ATTEND A GOVERNMENT** ceremony in 2006. Than Shwe handed over leadership of the Burmese armed forces to Maung Aye in 2006.

charge of each of more than thirty departments, from agriculture to defense to energy to livestock breeding and fisheries.

The country is divided into seven states, based primarily on the ethnicity of their inhabitants, and seven other divisions, based mostly on geography. Before 1988 there were local councils on the state, town, and village level, and local courts. However, after 8-8-88, the national government disbanded local organizations and took control of all levels of government. The government also controls the courts. Many of the court lawyers and judges are disinterested or even incompetent. Lawsuits are often settled with a bribe. A lawsuit against the state is virtually unwinnable.

SOURCES OF POWER

How has a man as insular, poorly educated, and superstitious as Than Shwe managed to stay in power? Unlike other Burmese leaders who forged links with other nations during college years or while fighting in one of the many wars that affected the country, Than Shwe has had little experience with the world outside Burma. This may have helped him. He has little desire to work with other countries—though his regime has developed profitable trade agreements with China and several Southeast Asian countries hungry for Burma's natural gas and oil. Because he does not rely on other countries in the West and the Pacific Rim—those countries bordering the Pacific Ocean—for trade, he is not disturbed when human rights groups urge sanctions against Burma. The United States and Canada have imposed sanctions that forbid investment in Burma, importation of Burmese goods, and export of goods and services into Burma. The United Nations, however, has hesitated to impose sanctions. This is in part because China, Burma's trading partner and a member of the UN Security Council (the arm of the UN responsible for maintaining international peace and security), objects strongly and in part, perhaps, because the UN feels sanctions have so far had little effect on the junta.

Than Shwe's paranoia about interference from the West and his ties to the army have led him to pour Burma's limited economic resources into the military. The government has neglected the country's infrastructure—its roads, bridges, and railroads—and its natural resources. Instead, it has used the money to increase the power and strength of the army. The number of military personnel leaped from 180,000 before 1988 to 480,000 in 2008. The government invested hundreds of millions of dollars in tanks, ships, and planes and in factories to make arms and ammunition.

Than Shwe rarely appears in public, and when he gives a speech, his words are dull and repetitive. He usually stresses the need for military readiness at all costs, focusing on what he sees as threats to Burma from outside and inside the nation, including frequent uprisings by dissident ethnic groups around the country. He and his regime are willing to use exile, forced labor, torture, and rape to punish rebels and keep the population under control. The buildup of the armed forces has allowed him to do just that.

THAN SHWE'S ARMY

The armed forces under Than Shwe are known as the Tatmadaw. The Tatmadaw is an elite force with its own schools, hospitals, and

"I was there [Mandalay Su Saun Yay, a military training camp] for fifteen days. They were asking children [to join the army] and beating them, they asked them one by one and then beat them with teak wood on the hips. Myself, I was afraid and just wished I could be with my parents. The first day I saw 250 taken to be asked. . . . The first day I was beaten seven times, and thirty times in my whole time there. Then I agreed to join, and they stopped beating me."

—Burmese boy, snatched off the streets, describing his first days in the Burmese army, 2002

banks. Nearly half of Burma's yearly budget goes to the army. Some estimates claim that 20 percent of the Tatmadaw are underage children, some of whom are snatched off the streets. Many of these children are orphans or have left their families, who cannot afford to feed and clothe them. However, they are not necessarily better off in the army, where they are subject to intimidation and beatings from officers, forced to do hard labor for little or no pay, and sent unprepared into battle.

CHAPTER 5

LIFE UNDER

RELIABLE FIGURES ON SOCIAL CONDITIONS IN BURMA are hard to come by, because of the government's secrecy and unwillingness to cooperate with international rights groups. The government has not taken a census since 1983. In 2008 the United Nations Development Programme ranked Burma 132 out of 177 nations on its Human Development Index. The index measures life expectancy, literacy, education, standard of living, and GDP, or gross domestic product—the value of goods and services produced within a nation's border in a given time. The average Burmese income was less than three hundred dollars a year in 2008, and over 70 percent of that income was spent on food. And in 2007, a group called Transparency International stated that Burma was the second most corrupt state in the world, after Somalia. This information reveals a country whose people are suffering.

THAN SHWE

THE BURMESE VILLAGER

The vast majority of Burmese, over 70 percent, live in rural areas. Most of them work in agriculture. They reside in small villages and work the surrounding fields, which are owned by the state. They practice subsistence farming, which means they are able to grow enough for their own use only. If there is extra, it is often bartered for other necessities. Many villages have a monastery, and the monks are the community's spiritual leaders. In return, the villagers give them the food and clothing they need to survive.

In the early 1960s, a typical villager grew rice, beans, cotton, or corn. Villages that grew rice generally did not grow other crops, since the fields had to be specially irrigated and other crops could not grow in the wet fields. In a rice village, the rice was planted after the first rains, usually in late spring or early summer. In July and August, the rice was transplanted to flooded fields, with farmers, both male and female, standing ankle deep in the water planting the delicate shoots. For the next four months, the farmers took care of other tasks, such as cutting firewood or preparing their household gardens. In December and January, farmers using scythes (sharp, curved knives) harvested the rice. It was threshed to separate the rice grains from the stalk. Then it was sold.

The village supported other businesses as well. There would often be a carpenter, a tailor—because all clothing was made in the village—and a storekeeper, who would sell goods needed by

A WOMAN POLES A BOAT FILLED WITH HARVESTED RICE THROUGH A BURMESE village on Inle Lake in 1962.

the villagers. A village might have had a concrete-floored school, if there were enough people to support it.

Villagers lived in thatched huts with bamboo sides. Often several generations lived under one roof in traditional Burmese fashion. Some huts had a cookhouse attached where meals were prepared. A villager's daily life might have begun at daybreak, when the husband or wife started the cookhouse fire. The family drank tea and ate a light breakfast, perhaps noodles in fish soup, which the women and young children served. Depending on the season, the family then did farmwork or chores. Some of the children attended school. Visits from family and neighbors were common throughout the day. In the evening, the family ate rice, soup, and curry (a spicy stew), prayed to the Buddha, and went to sleep, often in a single family bed.

Burmese village children were expected to respect their elders, and everyone in the village respected the monks. Forms of etiquette were very important and governed familial and social interaction. Villagers bowed or knelt to elders or monks. The head of the family was always served food first, even if the person was not present. Burmese have a great fear of embarrassing others, which they call *ahnarde*. This has led them to refrain from asking for favors, in case the person asked could not provide what was needed.

Under Than Shwe, village life changed drastically. His government has no official ideology (political philosophy). Its only aim appears to be complete control of the population and the consolidation of power in the hands of a few high-ranking generals. This aim is reflected in the Four Cuts policy. The intention of Four Cuts is to cut off food, funds, recruits, and information to groups opposing the government. Because there were so many ethnic groups and political organizations that objected to the regime's violent reaction to the uprising of 8-8-88, Than Shwe believes that every village holds a potential threat to his power. Deliberate destruction of villages and forced relocation of ethnic villagers, who make up at least 50 percent of the country's total population, is one way the government implements Four Cuts. Literally thousands of villages have been destroyed. All ethnic groups have been affected by the displacement policy—the Shan, Karenni, Kachin, Mon, and especially the Karen, who live in eastern Burma.

After the British granted independence to Burma in 1948, the Karen ethnic group asked for autonomy, or their own independent state within Burma. Their continued call for autonomy and the fact that Karen villages welcomed many who fled the cities after 8-8-88 are seen as a threat by the junta. Than Shwe's retaliation has been brutal. Karen villages have been singled out for forced relocation. At any moment, soldiers might surround a village. They will shoot guns and explode mortars, and burn rice paddies and houses. They loot homes and steal livestock, confiscating what they find for the army. Villagers who flee are shot. Those who remain are forced to move to a camp controlled by the army. Some villagers are made to work for the army as porters or as searchers for land mines. These workers are regularly beaten, raped, and starved.

A Buddhist monk born in 1957 grew up in a Karen farming village. He told how his village was attacked in 1997. He and his family were relocated, but he escaped to a monastery. He describes the current situation in the local village.

> The main problem in our area is that the *Tatmadaw* attack people, and villagers are unable to support themselves. They face food shortages, have less money, and have health care problems. For example, Saw Pah Lay was shot and killed by the *Tatmadaw* while he was harvesting in his paddy farm. . . . Another villager, Nay Pwe Moo Pah, trod on

a landmine and was killed. Battles took place in the area more than ten times.

Villagers who escape forced relocation often hide in the jungles or forests near their old villages. They eat what food they can find, sometimes growing rice in hidden fields. They try to organize religious and educational services when they can. But if they are found, the soldiers will kill them.

More than seven hundred thousand Karen have been displaced under Than Shwe. Many stay in refugee camps just over the border in Thailand, where some have lived for decades. The Thai government welcomed the refugees after 8-8-88, but the Thai government

CHILDREN WATCH AS A THAI SOLDIER PATROLS AT A REFUGEE SHELTER in Thailand near the Burmese border in 1997. The largest camps are home to as many as forty thousand people at a time.

has since found them a burden. Occasionally, they force groups of refugees to return to Burma. At other times, the Thais look away when the Burmese army crosses the border and attacks the camps. Children born in these camps have no citizenship and so later are unable to find work.

An eight-year-old Karen girl, Naw Paw Aye, lived in a Burmese village that was attacked in 1997. She and her family were forced to flee to a village called Mei Pya Po, which she recalls.

> All the people living in Mei Pya Po were strangers because all of these people came from other villages to seek refuge from the Burmese Army. . . . Mei Pya Po is located in a valley of a stream, and has no flatland. Some people plant crops on the slopes of the mountain. My parents prepared a paddy field in Ka Pler Hta with more than ten other families. We had to walk two hours from Mei Pya Po to get to the field. My father could walk without a problem, but it was a long walk for me.

Before long, though, the army attacked Mei Pya Po too. Naw Paw Aye tells what happened.

> I saw Burmese soldiers running around and shooting their guns. . . . After a long while, I heard my mother crying out. I saw one of the Burmese soldiers dragging her. In her hands, she was holding my little sister. I did not dare go and help my mother even though I saw her. I stayed hidden under that big tree. I saw my father go try to help my mother. The soldier shot him, and he fell down. I heard my mother cry out about two more times and then I never saw her again.

Naw Paw Aye went to live with her aunt in another small village, where the threat of attack is always present. She laments that there is no school in the village, saying, "I am longing for my schooling."

Even the villages that are not destroyed are surrounded by army units. These units demand one person per household to work as a laborer for the state. Villagers are forced to maintain army camps, run messages, grow food or dig fishponds for farming fish for the army, and make bricks for the soldiers. They work for a set period of time, and then they are replaced by new workers.

> *"They died from beatings after they couldn't manage the work—we had to carry heavy loads of wood through the mud and it was very difficult work. The bodies of the four men I saw die were thrown into the sea."*
>
> —Burmese worker forced to cultivate shrimp on the western coast of Burma, describing the death of his coworkers in 1994

When asked about the deaths of villagers, an army officer impassively explained to a reporter that they had trouble adjusting to a new climate. "They sweat a lot, they lose weight and they have some health problems," he stated. "Every day people are dying. It's a normal thing."

In 1994 there were more than three hundred thousand Burmese refugees in camps in Thailand, Bangladesh, India, and China. More than one million relocated villagers lived within Burma's borders. Those numbers have grown in the twenty-first century, though the government suppresses the true totals. It is obvious, however, that village life in Burma is quickly disappearing. Those villages that are not targeted for destruction or for the relocation of their inhabitants are fading more slowly. The army takes workers, seeds, and livestock from them, leaving the villagers with too little food and too few people to work the land.

The government has also forbidden the teaching of ethnic languages. Burmese is the language officially taught in school, and if students learn a second language, it is often English. The culture, oral traditions, and histories of Burma's ethnic groups, passed down in the dialects of Burma's many villages, are disappearing as the villages vanish.

LIFE IN THE CITY

There are several large cities in Burma. Rangoon has a population of four million, and Mandalay is home to more than two million people. Hundreds of thousands of Burmese live in smaller cities, such as Moulmein (changed to Mawlamyine) and Bassein (changed to Pathien). Many villagers fled to the cities of Burma when village life grew too dangerous. But city life, too, has become more and more difficult under Than Shwe's increasingly repressive regime. Families who flee their villages often have trouble finding housing in the city. They end up living in rickety shacks or rooms without windows, plumbing, or electricity. Even when they have power, electricity in Burma's cities is unreliable. It is often on only a few hours a day, since the government has neglected the country's infrastructure in order to sink its funds into the military.

While the typical worker in Rangoon makes twice the average national income, it is very expensive to live there. And it is getting more costly every day. Many families come to Rangoon in the hope of educating their children beyond the elementary level. They find that special school fees and uniform costs, required by the state, eat up half their monthly salary. They frequently fall into debt or are forced to cut back on food and other necessities.

SALARIES IN BURMA

In 2004 the average day laborer in Burma made the equivalent of about 19 cents a day or less than $6 a month. By contrast, the lowest salaried military personnel were paid about twice that. In 2006 the government gave civil servants (government workers) a huge raise. The lowest wage paid to military personnel rose to 80 cents a day. Senior General Than Shwe's salary rose from about $176 to approximately $920 a month, though he and other high-ranking military officers obviously have sources of income in addition to their salaries. Rumors claim that most government officials are involved in bribery, black marketeering, and the drug trade.

A Burmese taxi driver recently protested, "I hate my life here. I'm just surviving one day at a time. Everything's so difficult. Prices keep going up, and there is too little food and electricity. There are so many restrictions on everything I want to do . . . and so much corruption." He reported that he had to pay bribes at roadside checkpoints as he drove around the city. A taxi driver must have gasoline to make a living, but a Burmese citizen is allowed only 1 or 2 gallons (3.7 or 7.5 liters) of gas a day, and sometimes people must stand in line for hours to get those few gallons. The only alternative is the black market, where merchandise is bought and sold illegally. Goods such as gasoline sold on the black market are often twice as expensive—but at least they are available. In fact, much of the black market gasoline is sold by corrupt government officials and military officers, who are able to buy gasoline much more cheaply

DRIVERS WAIT FOR HOURS FOR FUEL AT A GOVERNMENT-RUN GAS STATION in Rangoon.

than other citizens and then turn around and sell it at a profit to those who must pay the price to keep their business going.

Other items sold on the black market include cars, which can cost as much as $16,000 for a used car and $250,000 for a sports utility vehicle, and cell phones, which cost more than $2,500. Few Burmese can afford these items, but many black market goods are sold across Burma's borders or to the few tourists who come into the country. Much of the money made on these items goes to the government, which requires registration for such luxuries, as well as bribes paid by those who buy and sell.

City dwellers complain that they must seek government permission for everything they do. Even having a family member from out of town spend the night requires authorization. All travel requires a permit. People fear informants, whom the government pays well. As a result, most citizens are very reserved in conversation, never knowing if what they say will be reported. Arrests can occur at any time.

THE DRUG TRADE IN BURMA

Only Afghanistan produces more opium, a narcotic made from the opium poppy, than Burma. As long ago as 3400 B.C., opium was used as a drug both for its narcotic and its medicinal effects in Mesopotamia (modern Iraq) and Egypt. It came to China about A.D. 400, and in the sixteenth century, farmers in Burma's Shan State began growing opium poppies. At first the opium they produced was used as medicine, but they soon found that the sale of opium for use as a narcotic to the Chinese was very profitable. When heroin, a stronger narcotic, began to be produced from opium, demand grew much greater, as did profits. Burma became known as part of the "Golden Triangle," a trio of opium-producing countries that included Thailand and Laos.

In 1962 Burma outlawed opium, and the drug went underground. Warlords (militia leaders) in the Shan State continued to export the drug in huge quantities, as the demand for it in Western nations grew. When the State Law and Order Restoration Council took power in Burma in 1988, opium production skyrocketed. While the government officially condemns the growth and sale of opium, many analysts assume that the junta has a hand in the huge amount of money generated by the drug trade. For the Burmese who grow the poppies, the official government condemnation has had little effect. They make so much more money from the opium crop than they could in any other way that they are willing to risk a government crackdown and, if it occurs, will simply shift their cultivation to another area.

AN OPIUM SELLER IN A BURMESE market holds a ball of raw opium wrapped in poppy leaves.

From 1998 to 2006, the Burmese government reported that the amount of opium in Burma decreased from more than 60 percent of all the opium produced in the world to less than 6 percent, due to government crackdowns and efforts by the United Nations and other international organizations. These numbers are nearly impossible to verify and may only indicate a movement in opium production from the Shan State to other areas in the country. In 2007 the United Nations noted that cultivation increased by 46 percent, once again making Burma the second-largest producer of opium.

THE LIVES OF MONKS

The monks of Burma hold a special place in society, even under Than Shwe's regime. The regime itself professes to be Buddhist, although its harsh and self-serving policies violate the most basic beliefs of the religion. Burmese people hold Buddhist monks in great reverence. Most boys will spend at least several months as novices, usually entering the monastery at about the age of seven. The time they spend in the monastery is considered a great privilege. They shave their heads and put on maroon robes as their families celebrate in a village ceremony that includes dancing and feasting. The novice agrees to obey the ten precepts of Buddhism. Some of the boys will stay on to acquire an education. Others will stay for good, renouncing all material wealth, receiving a new name, and putting on the maroon robes of a monk for the rest of their lives.

Older men also may become monks. Some may come from wealthier families and want to renounce the material world. Others may want to retire from work. Still others may come from families where becoming a monk is a tradition. There are between three hundred thousand and five hundred thousand monks in Burma. One out of every hundred boys or men is a monk.

Women can become Buddhist nuns, but it is far less common. A woman usually joins a nunnery because her husband or son has died, or she is in debt. Nuns shave their heads and wear pink robes, and they lead religious ceremonies and work to teach and spread Buddhism throughout the land. Only rarely will a nun actually preach, as the Burmese value modesty among women. When nuns beg as monks do for their daily food, they cannot go alone. Nuns are respected in society, as monks are, but they are below monks on the social ladder.

As spiritual leaders of the people, Burma's monks have been in the forefront of antigovernment protests since the time of British rule. Their protests began in the late 1920s against British colonials who refused to remove their shoes when they entered sacred Buddhist pagodas, purposely showing disrespect for Buddhism. In the first uprising in 1929, two monks, U Wisara and U Ottama, were arrested by the British and U Wisara died in prison after a 166-day hunger strike.

TWO BUDDHIST NUNS PRAY AT the Shwedagon Pagoda in Rangoon in 2008.

One monk explained their role as the voice of the Burmese people, saying, "When Burmese people suffer, normally they don't dare to speak out. So we express their suffering for them." In 1988 the monks helped lead the antigovernment protests, as they did

SPIRITUAL PUNISHMENT

Monks have a very powerful weapon to use against those whom they consider to have betrayed the tenets of Buddhism. It's called *pattam nik-kujana kamma*, which means "turning the bowl." When the monks are approached by an almsgiver they think is not behaving properly, they literally turn their alms bowls upside down. This denies the almsgiver the opportunity to earn spiritual merit by giving to the monks, and it is considered a terrible punishment. The monks used this weapon against the junta's soldiers in 2007.

again in 2007. The junta's attacks on the monks in 2007 were deeply shocking to the Burmese people, who continue to treat them with the greatest respect. Since the uprising, many monks have been imprisoned, trapped inside their monasteries, or closely watched by government forces.

HEALTH CARE IN BURMA

Widespread poverty in Burma has led to an ever-growing health crisis throughout the country. There are not many doctors—fewer than one for each three thousand people. The maternal mortality rate—or percentage of women who die from childbirth-related causes—is very high, as is the infant mortality rate—the percentage of children who die before their first birthday. Many children are malnourished. As the rate of spending on health care by the government goes down, the rate of serious illness climbs. As of 2009, only about 3 percent of total yearly spending went to health care—about forty cents per person.

Life expectancy in Burma is only 62 years, as opposed to 82 in Japan and 78 in the United States. Malaria and dengue fever, illnesses spread by mosquitoes, are huge problems. There are high rates of the infectious lung disease tuberculosis, waterborne dysentery and typhoid, and measles. HIV/AIDS is a serious problem, with over 3 million people estimated to be infected.

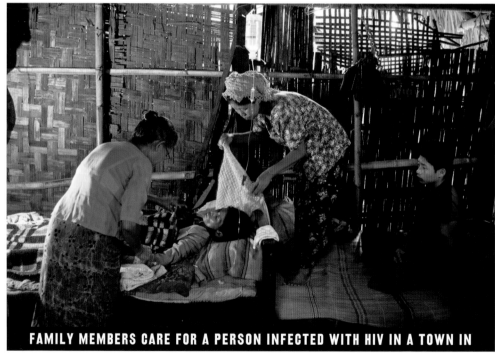

FAMILY MEMBERS CARE FOR A PERSON INFECTED WITH HIV IN A TOWN IN northern Burma. A shortage of doctors and AIDS educators has made it almost impossible to treat HIV/AIDS patients or stop the spread of the virus in Burma.

Reasons for the health problems that are rampant in Burma go beyond poverty. The guerrilla warfare by dissident ethnic groups that rages along the country's borders and the forced relocation of villagers has cut off many Burmese from access to health care. Poor sanitation and bad water quality also lead to disease outbreaks. A high number of intravenous drug users and sex workers in Burma's cities has led to the spread of HIV/AIDS.

Though there are few Burmese doctors, many aid groups have been allowed to send doctors and establish clinics throughout the country. The World Health Organization, an agency of the UN, works with the Burmese Ministry of Health on various health problems throughout the country. Doctors Without Borders (an international medical organization) has been a presence in the country for many years in areas with little access to health care.

EDUCATION UNDER THAN SHWE

Burmese law requires children to go to school through the fourth grade. However, the government does not fund schools adequately and requires students to pay fees many families cannot afford. Nearly 40 percent of children never even start school. Of those who go, fewer than one-third get to fourth grade. Dropout rates in upper grades are also high.

Schools run by Buddhist monasteries try to close the educational gaps, and they provide schooling for disadvantaged children and orphans. Poor rural families are the least likely to send children to school. They often need their older children to work to bring money into the home. Boys who leave school are at risk of being forced

BURMESE CHILD SOLDIERS AWAIT INSPECTION AT THEIR DORMITORY NEAR THE Thai border. These boys were recruited into the army of a Burmese drug lord.

into the military. Children as young as eleven years old have been recruited, and in the twenty-first century, army recruiters have used force, such as threats and beatings, to recruit children.

The government closed colleges and universities in Burma from 1996 to 2000 because of the antigovernment demonstrations led or fueled by students. During this time, the military established universities and technical schools for the children of military officers. These institutions were funded by the state education budget. When the public colleges and universities reopened, there was a huge influx of students who had been waiting to start or return to college. Classes were overcrowded, courses were shortened, and students were rushed through the system. University students are watched closely by police and government informers to prevent further protests.

THE BURMESE ENVIRONMENT

Burma is rich in natural resources. It has vast deposits of oil and natural gas. Underground, there are rubies, gold, silver, tin, and jade. The soil of the Irrawaddy Delta is very fertile, and the country's forests produce valuable teak and mahogany. The wildlife of Burma is varied, from endangered tigers and elephants to snakes and turtles. Gradually, though, this rich legacy is being destroyed.

In 1994 the junta stated the following in its National Environmental Policy:

> The wealth of the nation is its people, its cultural heritage, its environment and its natural resources. The objective of Myanmar's environmental policy is aimed at achieving harmony and balance between these through the integration of environmental considerations into the development process to enhance the quality of life of all its citizens. . . . It is the responsibility of the State and every citizen to preserve its natural resources in the interests of present and future generations.

The government's actions do not support its policy. Unregulated timber cutting has greatly damaged the teak forests. Only 30 percent of Burma remains forested, down from 57 percent in 1960, and the country is losing up to 1.5 percent of its remaining forests each year. The rate of deforestation, or loss of woodlands, has doubled since Than Shwe came into power. This creates soil erosion, flooding, and threats to wildlife. Mining releases toxins into the soil and water. Dams built across the country's largest rivers slow water flow,

BLACK MARKET ANIMALS

There is a huge black market (illegal) demand for Burma's rare animals. In the Chinese border town of Mong La, you can find elephant tusks, tiger and leopard skins, and cages holding pangolins, macaques, pythons, and star tortoises, many of which will be cooked and eaten by Chinese buyers. Mong La, in fact, has become what is called the Vegas of the East, with casinos filled with Chinese gamblers, houses of prostitution, and a thriving drug trade. Much of the profit made here goes into the hands of Burmese military officials.

threatening aquatic plants and animals and lowering water quality. Factories spew waste into the air and water.

Burma has more than a dozen national parks and wildlife sanctuaries, including the world's largest tiger sanctuary. Even those areas are not well protected. Logging and poaching are continual threats to the wildlife in the parks. Experts estimate that nearly one hundred animal species and forty plant species are threatened or endangered in Burma.

THE JUNTA AND THE PRESS

One of the hallmarks of a repressive government is restriction of the press. Burma is no exception to this rule. The reason the outside world knows so little about Burma is that the junta has extremely tight control of all media within the country. The government of Burma claims a surprisingly high literacy rate of 83 percent of the population, though this has not been verified. Regardless of how many Burmese are able to read, the people are severely limited in what they can read.

Before 1962 Burma had an active free press. When Ne Win took over, however, journalists' organizations were banned, and many journalists were arrested. Foreign reporters were thrown out of the country. The government regulated all information, nationalizing the newspapers and setting up a press scrutiny board to censor publications.

As unrest spread in 1988, rebels began putting out underground newspapers and other publications. When the State Law and Order Restoration Council took over in 1988, they forced these journals to close, and reporters had to flee for their lives.

Burma has four official daily newspapers, all published by a division of the government's Information Ministry. These publications contain government press releases, articles from international press sources that report negatively on countries critical of Burma, and cartoons that ridicule the NLD. The government blocks news about problems in Burma, from political corruption to drug trafficking and even Burmese sports teams that lose their international matches.

One newspaper that claims to be independent, the *Myanmar Times*, is not regulated as closely as other papers. It is published weekly by an Australian journalist, Ross Dunkley, who lives in Rangoon. The paper has reported on political issues, such as talks with the NLD and the army's use of forced labor. Many international analysts believe that the paper is controlled by a government group that hopes to improve the junta's image abroad. However, in January 2008, the junta temporarily stopped publication of the newspaper because without permission it included an article on the government raising fees for satellite television.

TRICYCLE DRIVERS, WHO PROVIDE TAXI SERVICE IN RANGOON, READ newspapers in English and Burmese in 2007.

The Committee to Protect Journalists, a nonprofit organization based in New York, names Burma, along with Indonesia, as the Asian nation most hostile to media. Many Burmese journalists have spent years in prison. One claimed, "If you haven't been in jail, you haven't been a reporter here." The committee reports that currently seven journalists are in prison in Burma and notes that one Japanese reporter was killed by soldiers in the 2007 uprising. Reporters Without Borders, another nonprofit organization, claims at least nineteen media writers are in prison in Burma.

Many Burmese reporters have moved to Thailand, where they continue to write about their country. They produce articles on the ethnic warfare along the Burmese borders and describe the situation of Burmese refugees. The Thai government refuses to grant these journalists Thai travel documents. Like the Burmese refugees in Thailand, they have no country.

The *Irrawaddy* is the best-known Burmese magazine to come out of Thailand. It is run by Aung Zaw, who fled to Thailand after 8-8-88. The magazine reports, often critically, on all aspects of Burmese life and politics. It is available online, but few Burmese have ever seen it. The Mizzima News Group also publishes online and has an Internet television station that provides news and information about Burma, but again, few Burmese have access to it.

Newsletters put out by the Shan and Karen independence groups and by the NLD circulate within Burma, but those caught reading them risk imprisonment. A number of weekly and monthly papers and magazines are published in Burma as well. While not official government bulletins, they are heavily censored and regulated by the government, which holds their publishing licenses. Every edition of every publication goes to the Press Scrutiny Board. Censors decide which articles must be cut. Sometimes publishers can bribe the censors to allow publication if the article in question is about a minor problem.

Radio and television services for Burma also operate both within and outside the country. The interior media is censored, and the two television stations and eight radio stations are state run. In 2001 fewer than eight people per thousand had a television and one in ten had a radio. This has changed somewhat since then. More Burmese have purchased satellite dishes that allow them to view foreign television. Outside the country, the Democratic Voice of Burma and Radio Free Asia bring information about Burma to the rest of the world and try to get word of international affairs to the Burmese.

One in one thousand Burmese had a computer in 2001, and almost none of them had Internet access. By 2006 the government had permitted sixteen Internet cafés to open, but the content was strictly controlled both in public cafés and at home. Later that year, the government cut off access to Gmail, Hotmail, Google, and Internet telephone service. After the 2007 uprising, Internet access was even more drastically restricted. In Internet cafés, computer users are prohibited from viewing foreign websites, but café workers are skilled in helping them find their way around the ban. The *New York Times* reported that when users sign off, they are instructed to erase their download history so the government cannot trace it. The group Reporters Without Borders calls Burma one of fifteen "black holes in the Internet."

Though satellite television and the Internet allow Burmese increased access to the outside world, the number who benefit from these changes is very small. Pe Thet Nee, the editor at the Burmese Independent News Agency, based in Thailand, described the effect of the restrictions on information this way. "To me it is mental genocide. They are not killing the Burmese people physically but they are killing our ability to think."

BURMESE JUSTICE

When limiting information by suppression and censorship is not enough, Than Shwe's regime turns to the courts. In 1974 Burma's constitution merged the judicial and the lawmaking parts of the government. This gives the current regime the power to appoint Supreme Court justices. In turn, the Supreme Court chooses judges for the lower courts, subject to the junta's approval. All courts, therefore—town, district, state, and national—are effectively run by the junta.

The state police can arrest anyone at any time on orders of the government. Once in the system, a political prisoner has little or no way out. A prisoner can be held for three years without a trial. He or she is likely to disappear—for months, years, or forever.

In 2005 a group based in Thailand called the Assistance Association for Political Prisoners published a document titled *The Darkness We See: Torture in Burma's Interrogation Centers and Prisons*. In great detail, it describes the way political prisoners— those who openly disagree with or are thought to disagree with the junta's policies—are treated.

After 8-8-88 the junta approved the use of military tribunals, or courts, to try dissidents. These courts run their trials inside prisons. They don't require witnesses or give defendants access to lawyers. There is no right of appeal for a sentence given by a tribunal. The tribunals can give three sentences: not less than three years' imprisonment with labor, life imprisonment, or death.

TORTURE THE BURMESE WAY

Torturers in Burmese prisons have several special procedures, which are described in *The Darkness We See*. One procedure, called the Iron Road, consists of rolling an iron rod up and down a prisoner's shins, ripping off the skin. Another is called the Semigwa Dance, which is the name of a traditional Burmese dance. In this form of torture, prisoners must crawl on gravel on their knees and elbows while singing.

Since 1988 between five and ten thousand Burmese have been arrested and held as political prisoners, often on very weak grounds. As of 2007, nearly two thousand were still imprisoned. They are not told of the charges against them until their trials, which are held in junta-run courts. They do not have lawyers and are not allowed to see their families.

Before trial the prisoners are usually handcuffed, shackled, or tied down. After days without food, adequate water, or sleep, they are questioned. Often they are kept in dark cells.

"When they closed the door, there was no light in the cell. That's why it was called the pitch-black cell. Furthermore, there was no bamboo mat, no blanket, and no chamber pot. . . . A few hours later, I was scared and shaking. Coldness, darkness, and loneliness attacked me in the cell."

—Burmese prisoner describing his imprisonment, 2005

Prisoners routinely undergo torture, including beatings, near drownings, and electric shocks. Their interrogators blindfold them or place hoods over their faces, making it difficult to breathe. They are deprived of sleep, forced to kneel on glass, or hung by the arms or feet. Authorities also threaten prisoners and their families and friends. One prisoner stated, "They said they had the right to kill us, stop our visits with our families, and keep us in jail for a long time."

After a trial, which usually ends in a guilty verdict, prisoners are placed in cells that they share with rats, mice, fleas, snakes, lice, and flies. Those who complain about conditions may be put in solitary confinement, tortured, or transferred to another prison. One prisoner who complained got some satisfaction but at a severe price.

> While in Tharrawaddy [a prison outside Rangoon], some political prisoners and I went on a 3 day hunger strike to demand the authorities provide prisoners with better rice. The hunger strike was successful and we were finally given better quality rice, although I would later learn that such an action had caused the authorities to extend my prison sentence.

Most prison food features poor-quality rice and curries made mostly of water. Sometimes prisoners find sand or stones mixed in. They are given beef, pork, fish, or eggs only once a week. If relatives are allowed to visit, they may bring extra food, but for many families it is difficult to visit prisoners because of the distance or government discouragement.

The prison cells are filthy, and prisoners drink dirty water. Many become very ill, but doctors rarely visit. When prisoners receive injections, the authorities reuse needles, a common way to spread HIV. HIV travels easily within the prison population.

PRISONS IN BURMA

There are thirty-nine prisons in Burma that house political prisoners. The vast majority of these prisons are in the Irrawaddy Delta region, but others are scattered all over the country. Amnesty International has identified twenty sites in Burma where torture is routinely practiced. In Mae Sot, on the Burma-Thailand border, Bo Kyi *(below)*, a Burmese exile and former prisoner, has built a replica of a Burmese prison cell that has become a museum. In it, he displays maps of Burmese prisons, biographies and pictures of prisoners, descriptions of torture devices, and carvings and writings done by political prisoners within Burma.

When political prisoners are released after serving their sentences, they often suffer both physical and psychological problems for years. They may have nerve damage or spinal cord injuries from beatings. They may have contracted tuberculosis or AIDS in prison. Many suffer from post-traumatic stress disorder, which causes depression, nightmares, and other psychological problems. Even those who are not harmed in any lasting way have trouble reentering their old lives. As one released prisoner explains, "When released, I felt marginalized [left out] by society as my friends were afraid to meet with me. In fact, only one of my old friends came to visit me after prison."

There are over 150 female political prisoners, and nearly two hundred monks. One political prisoner, journalist U Win Tin, had been in prison since 1989 and was only released in September 2008, at nearly eighty years old. He suffered two heart attacks in jail but refused to give up his membership in the NLD in return for his freedom. In 2001 he was awarded the UNESCO/Guillermo Cano World Press Freedom Prize and the World Association of Newspapers' Golden Pen of Freedom Award. Even from prison, his presence was felt and his voice was heard.

CHAPTER 6

BURMA

BURMA IS CLOSED TO MUCH OF THE WORLD, both because of the government's isolationist policies and the sanctions many countries have put in place. However, Burma has close ties to a number of countries in Southeast Asia. It is a member both of the Bay of Bengal Initiative for Multi-Sectoral Technical and Economic Cooperation (BIMSTEC) and of the Association of Southeast Asian Nations (ASEAN). It trades freely with the countries in those groups. ASEAN has recently refused to defend Burma when its human rights record is discussed at international meetings, revealing a growing sense of unease with the regime. Nevertheless, the group retains its trade agreements with Burma, hoping to influence the country positively and weaken its economic and political ties with China.

Burma is rich in oil, which it sells to its trade partners. The

AND THE **W**ORLD

THAN SHWE ATTENDS A MEETING of the Association of Southeast Asian Nations in Indonesia in 1996. That year he asked for Burma's membership in the association.

country imports relatively little from other countries, so it has a surplus in foreign trade. The oil fields are controlled by the government, which reaps the profits from the sale of oil. In addition to oil, Burma exports natural gas, teak, gems, and rubber. It imports food, machinery, and manufactured goods, but much of the population never sees these products. They go primarily to members of the government or military.

Much of Burma's trade is with the People's Republic of China. Burma was the first non-Communist country to recognize China after the takeover by the Communist regime in 1949, and Burma and China signed a treaty in 1954. China's relations with Burma include the sale of arms to the junta, which Than Shwe's government uses to control the ethnic rebellions within its borders. Most manufactured goods in Burma are made in China. In return, Burma has agreed to build pipelines to carry oil and gas directly into China. Trade between the two countries increased by nearly 40 percent in 2007. Increasingly reliant on Burmese oil and gas as its own economy expands, China is also Burma's greatest ally in the UN. It has used its veto power to block criticism of and sanctions against the junta. China gives debt relief, or reduced payments on loans, to Burma and provides loans and grants to Burmese companies.

THE FIVE PRINCIPLES OF PEACEFUL COEXISTENCE

The relationship between Burma and the People's Republic of China is formally based on the Five Principles of Peaceful Coexistence. These include mutual respect for each other's borders and the right to control their people, mutual nonaggression, mutual noninterference in each other's internal affairs, equality, and mutual aid.

IN 1996 WORKERS BEGAN CONSTRUCTION OF A PIPELINE TO CARRY NATURAL gas from Burma to a power plant in Thailand. The government forced villagers to work to clear a path through the forest for the 256-mile-long (412 km) pipeline.

India and Thailand also offer Burma loans and debt relief in exchange for favorable conditions when purchasing imports. Their relations, however, are strained by border conflicts and by illegal drug trade. Much of the opium produced in Burma finds its way into India, Thailand, and China. Since Thailand is increasingly dependent on Burma for its supply of natural gas, the country is not in a position to protest strongly against the drug trade. In 2007 Burma exported $2.7 million worth of natural gas to Thailand, mostly through a pipeline that runs across the border directly from its offshore reserves.

India, too, benefits from Burma's gas and oil reserves and has invested heavily in them. In exchange, the Indian government has provided weapons for the regime and aims for $1 billion in trade with Burma. India's cooperation with and investment in Burma reflects its view of the country not only as a source of petroleum and natural gas but as a gateway to the expanding markets of Southeast Asia.

BURMA AND THE UNITED NATIONS

Burma's relationship with the United Nations is troubled, though the UN has not placed sanctions on the country. Early in the history of the UN, after World War II, Burma was a strong supporter. It was also one of the first countries to recognize Israel in 1948. U Thant, a Burmese, served as secretary-general, or leader of the UN, for two terms, from 1961 to 1971. However, the UN's support of Chinese nationalist Taiwan in 1949, when Chinese nationalist troops fighting the mainland Chinese were based in the Burmese highlands, led to uneasiness in the relationship. Since 8-8-88 the UN has strongly urged Burma's government to end its human rights abuses.

In 1993 a group of five Nobel Peace Prize winners appealed to the UN to suspend Burma from the organization. The group included South African archbishop Desmond Tutu, Costa Rican Oscar Arias Sanchez, Mairead Maguire and Betty Williams from Northern Ireland, and Argentine Adolpho Pérez Esquival. They asked the UN to place Burma under an arms embargo, forbidding shipments of weapons to the country, until the government released its political prisoners, ended human rights abuses, and recognized the results of the 1990 elections. However, the UN Security Council was strongly pressured by member country China and did not respond.

The UN's strongest response yet to Burma came after the September 2007 uprising. At that time, the Security Council passed a statement "strongly deploring" the violence against protesters by the government. However, the statement was nonbinding, and China kept the council from imposing sanctions.

The UN sent a special envoy, Ibrahim Gambari, a Nigerian professor and diplomat, to meet with Than Shwe and Aung San Suu Kyi

THAN SHWE *(LEFT)* **GREETS UN SPECIAL ENVOY IBRAHIM GAMBARI**
(right) at a 2006 meeting on human rights in Burma. The meeting, which included
Maung Aye *(center)*, took place in Naypyidaw.

in 2006, 2007, and early 2008. His task was to demand an end to
the killings sparked by the antigovernment protests and to request
the release of political prisoners, in particular Aung San Suu Kyi.
After his visits in 2007, he described his experience to a *Newsweek*
reporter. He stated that when he relayed these demands, Than Shwe
"was, of course, taken aback because they're pretty isolated. They
were somewhat surprised about how the world thinks of them."

Gambari feels some hope about the possibility of changing the
junta's behavior toward its people. He believes that if sanctions "are
combined with real engagement and some incentives at the appro-
priate time, they could work." Despite Gambari's condemnation
of the violence in his report to the Security Council, the junta has
continued to allow him to enter the country and hold talks with top

THE UNITED NATIONS SECURITY COUNCIL

There are five permanent members of the UN Security Council: the United States, China, the United Kingdom, the Federation of Russia, and France. In addition, there are ten nonpermanent members. These are elected by the General Assembly of all the member countries for a term of two years and cannot be reelected immediately. Decisions require at least nine of the fifteen members voting yes, and decisions on matters declared of substance require nine yes votes including all five of the permanent members. The other branches of the United Nations must accept and carry out the Security Council's decisions.

government officials. Gambari also visits neighboring countries, including Indonesia, Thailand, and China. His aim is to win their support for his efforts to convince the regime to loosen its repressive grip on the people of Burma.

INTERNATIONAL RESPONSES

Burma's relationship with the European Union (EU), a group consisting of twenty-seven European countries, has worsened since 2007. The EU has placed an embargo on arms sales to Burma, a ban on nonhumanitarian aid, sanctions on imports from Burma, and bans on various types of investment in the country. The EU issued a condemnation of the violence against the 2007 uprising. Still, the EU countries have not developed a unified foreign policy on Burma, and significant amounts of money and goods flow in and out of Burma from EU countries.

Relations between Burma and the United States have steadily worsened since 8-8-88, when the United States downgraded its representation in Burma (from ambassador to chargé d'affaires) to protest the violence. The United States passed the Burma Freedom and Democracy Act in 2003, banning imports from Burma and financial services to the country. In 2007, after the uprising in September, the U.S. government seized the assets that Burmese government officials had in the United States and forbade new U.S. investment in Burma. The United States has also designated Burma a Country of Particular Concern because of its limits on religious freedom, both in its harsh treatment of Buddhist monks who demonstrate against the government and in its repression of Muslim and Christian groups. It has condemned the Burmese regime for its use of forced labor.

Even so, companies in both the United States and the European Union—specifically, France—have managed to get around the sanctions against Burma. A group that includes the gas and oil companies Total, owned by France, and Unocal, a U.S. company later acquired by Chevron, has invested heavily in a Burmese gas pipeline. The Yadana Pipeline, completed in 1998, runs for 256 miles (412 km) from offshore Burma to Thailand. The organization EarthRights International states that work done on the pipeline endangers rare local wildlife and has destroyed much of the environment nearby. A lawsuit brought against Unocal in 1999 by a group of Burmese citizens claimed that thousands of Burmese were forced to relocate to make way for the pipeline and were beaten and killed by troops if they resisted. The lawsuit was settled in 2005, but the details of the settlement were not disclosed. Both Chevron and Total remain involved in the pipeline and its profits.

CHAPTER 7

WATCHING

THE YEAR 2007 PROVED TO BE A DIFFICULT ONE both for Than Shwe and for Burma. In January, news agencies began reporting that Than Shwe had left the country and had checked into a hospital in Singapore. Rumors flew that he was suffering from intestinal, prostate, or pancreatic cancer. A photographer who took pictures at the hospital was forced to delete them, and reporters were barred from the hospital. When Than Shwe missed the January 4 Independence Day celebrations for the first time since taking power, the rumors grew even wilder. However, the dictator was soon back in Burma, revealing no signs of health problems on the rare occasions when he was seen publicly.

In August 2007, the government made its fateful decision to raise oil prices, and the protests against the junta began. From a few hundred protesters marching in Rangoon on August 19, the

AND WAITING

demonstrations grew. What began as protests against a hike in fuel costs quickly became a protest against all the repressive policies of the military dictatorship.

THE SAFFRON REVOLUTION

On September 21, a group calling itself the Alliance of All Burmese Buddhist Monks issued a statement. In it they promised to continue protesting against the government, which they referred to as "the enemy of the people," until it was "wiped . . . from the land of Burma." The protest movement was known as the Saffron Revolution, after the deep yellow color of monks' robes in most of

Southeast Asia (though in Burma they are more often maroon). The monks announced that they would stop taking donations from military personnel, which was a powerful statement of condemnation. It meant that soldiers would not earn the spiritual credit that comes from donating to monks.

On September 22, ten thousand monks marched in Mandalay. In Rangoon a large number marched as well, and Aung San Suu Kyi came to her front gate to greet them as they passed by. On September 23, one hundred Buddhist nuns, dressed in pink robes, joined the march, and on September 24, a rally of one hundred thousand Burmese people, led by monks, gathered to protest the junta's actions. By this time, the outside world had begun to realize what was happening. Photographs taken on cell phones were sent from the streets of Rangoon to the major cities of the world. Videos of the demonstrations made their way onto the Internet. On September 25, the government banned public gatherings. They cut off Internet and cell phone service throughout the country and moved in to

MONKS LEAD THOUSANDS OF protesters on a peaceful march through the streets of Rangoon on September 24, 2007.

stop the demonstrations. Nonetheless, millions viewed the violence that ensued over the next two days, as the few Burmese who had access to cell or Internet service managed to get out photographs and videos that told the shocking story. Censure by nation after nation followed, but the regime did not back down. The United States and the European Union tightened sanctions, and the United Nations asked ASEAN to use its influence on the junta.

"The soldiers shouted to open the monastery gates, and then broke the gate by hitting it with their truck when no one came to open. Shouting loudly, they were throwing teargas and firing their automatic guns into the buildings of the monastery, and they used their batons to beat the monks whenever they saw them. Many monks ran away, climbing into the trees nearby. . . . I was injured in the head when I was hit by baton charges. I saw pools of blood, shattered windows, and spent bullet casings on the floor when I came back to the monastery in the morning. We found about 100 monks missing out of 230 monks."

—Burmese monk, describing the raid on his monastery in September 2007

In October the junta began to show signs of relenting in response to the constant pressure from other nations. UN envoy Ibrahim Gambari met with Than Shwe and with Aung San Suu Kyi. The government then appointed its labor minister, Aung Kyi, as a special minister of relations between the junta and the National League for Democracy. The junta permitted Aung Kyi to hold official talks with Aung San Suu Kyi, though no record of what they discussed was released. Aung San Suu Kyi was also allowed to meet with members of the NLD for the first time in over three years. She stated that she was willing to work with the junta, saying, "In the interest of the nation, I stand ready to cooperate with the government in order to make this process of dialogue a success."

Early in 2008, the junta, under both internal and external pressure, announced that it would invest its resources in the seven-step road map to democracy that General Khin Nyunt, arrested in 2004, had initially proposed in 2003. The steps consist of the constitutional convention, which did meet from 1993 until 2007, and the drafting of a new constitution, finally completed in early 2007. They also include the adoption of the constitution through a national referendum, "free and fair" elections, the meeting of elected officials, and the creation of government bodies by the elected legislature.

The referendum on the constitution was scheduled for May 10, 2008. However, the two-hundred-page constitution itself, fourteen years in the making, was created without the input of dissident groups. It included a guarantee for the military to hold 25 percent of the seats in parliament and a clause that would permit detention of prisoners without trial for up to five years. If adopted, the constitution would ensure that Aung San Suu Kyi would never be permitted to hold elected office and that the military would continue to rule the country. The possibility of free and fair elections under the

REPRESENTATIVES FROM BURMA'S ETHNIC MINORITY GROUPS ATTEND THE final meeting of the national constitutional convention in Nyaunghnapin in 2007.

constitution seemed unlikely. As the chief human rights investigator for the UN, Paolo Pinheiro, said, "If you believe in gnomes, trolls and elves, you can believe in this democratic process in Myanmar."

As the date for the referendum came closer, the government banned writing and speech that criticized the constitution. According to the *Irrawaddy,* the junta began sending officials throughout the country, using both threats and bribes to try to guarantee yes votes. In one township, the people were promised electricity and a new school if they voted yes and told their water supply would be cut off if they voted no. The government threatened a sentence of twenty years in prison if anyone spoke out against the referendum.

A week before the referendum, the UN Security Council issued a statement that urged the regime to make the upcoming vote "credible and inclusive." Though some members of the council had wanted to make its statement stronger, urging the release of political prisoners including Aung San Suu Kyi, other council members, led by China, insisted on weakening the language. Nevertheless, the statement was strong enough to invoke a harsh response from the Burmese government. The Burmese representative to the UN, Kyaw Tint Swe, called the statement "unprecedented." He insisted,

> Myanmar is not a threat to either international or regional peace and security, a fact testified to by all of Myanmar's neighbors and the Non-Aligned Movement [a group of 118 nations that are not formally aligned with any major powers] which constitute a clear majority of the UN membership.

CYCLONE NARGIS

On April 28, 2008, weather forecasters began tracking a tropical storm called a cyclone that was gaining strength in the Bay of Bengal. At first it appeared to be headed toward India, but it took an unexpected turn toward Burma. India issued warnings to the Burmese government, but either the junta did not broadcast them or the warnings came too late. On May 3, a week before the referendum, the cyclone called Nargis roared up the Irrawaddy Delta with terrible ferocity, taking a path few had originally predicted.

The Irrawaddy Delta, where the majority of Burma's 48 million people live, is filled with towns and villages of houses built of flimsy bamboo and corrugated tin. Nargis, with winds of over 120 miles (193 km) per hour, swept the houses away, destroying entire towns and

WHAT IS A CYCLONE?

A cyclone is a severe storm that forms over an ocean. A tropical cyclone is one that forms in the Indian Ocean. The same kind of storm is called a typhoon when it forms over the Pacific Ocean and a hurricane when it forms over the Atlantic. To be called a tropical cyclone, a storm must have winds that blow at more than 74 miles (120 km) per hour. It requires ocean temperatures of at least 80°F (27°C) and low atmospheric pressure, which helps pull moisture upward. Winds in cyclones spin in a clockwise direction in the Southern Hemisphere and counterclockwise in the Northern Hemisphere. Cyclones and hurricanes are classified by categories, with 1 being the weakest and 5 the strongest. Cyclone Nargis was a Category 4 storm when it hit land in Burma. "Nargis" is the Urdu word for daffodil.

killing untold numbers of people. An enormous storm surge rose up to 12 feet (3.7 m) high, and the ocean swept 25 miles (40 km) inland. The storm cut off electricity in the country. Fallen trees and floodwaters blocked roads into the delta region. The area's rice paddies, the food for most of Burma's population, were covered with seawater.

The first reports to come out of Burma, on Monday, May 5, claimed that more than 350 people were killed, with thousands more left homeless. Countries all over the world immediately offered food and medical supplies, but the junta did not respond. Over the next few days, evidence of the cyclone's incredible destruction began to surface. People posted photographs on the Internet of flooded villages with floating bodies of people and animals. The few international news reporters in Burma, who worked undercover because of the government's strict rules forbidding foreign news organizations, sent out reports of widespread death and devastation. Death tolls mounted day by day. Even the government's official tolls climbed into the tens of thousands, while the International Red Cross began estimating the number of dead at over one hundred thousand.

"In Laputta, 75–80% of the town has been destroyed. Most of the houses have the roofs blown out and smashed. . . . Out of town, sixteen villages along the coast have been virtually wiped out. They say nobody is helping."

–Laputta Township resident, Irrawaddy, an eyewitness to the aftermath of Cyclone Nargis, 2008

The United States offered to send large amounts of food and medicine, which were available in the area due to a naval exercise going on at the time. According to some reports, though, the U.S. government demanded oversight of the distribution of U.S. aid and observation of conditions in the delta. The junta, unwilling to allow foreign interference, refused and also rebuffed other foreign personnel who offered to help assess the damage and distribute the aid.

Days passed, and television and newspapers showed images of Burmese villagers, homeless and starving. Many people had

RESIDENTS OF BOGALAY, BURMA, SALVAGE BELONGINGS FROM HOUSES destroyed by Cyclone Nargis.

lost entire families, even their whole villages. One sixty-five-year-old woman, Kyin Hla, lost twelve members of her family, including her grandchildren, who were torn from her by the storm surge. Thousands of others had similar stories.

As governments around the world criticized the junta for blocking the distribution of desperately needed donations of food, water, clothing, and medical supplies waiting on planes and ships, Than Shwe and his government restated their insistence that outside observers would not be allowed in. They released photographs and videos of soldiers handing out rice and other supplies to villagers. At the same time, some unofficial reports claimed that few of the needy were receiving help, while others reported that distribution was taking place. Huge areas of the country were unreachable without the boats and helicopters offered by other nations.

Stagnant waters pooled in villages, and floating bodies began to decompose. The fear of disease outbreaks grew. The Burmese had no clean water. Cholera and typhoid—diseases spread by contaminated water—threatened, and the standing water bred mosquitoes that spread malaria.

On May 10, even though much of the country was in a state of panic and many people were without food, water, or shelter, the government held its constitutional referendum as planned. It postponed the vote in some of the areas hardest hit by the cyclone, but even so, many Burmese could not get to voting locations. The government announced on May 15 that the constitution was approved by more than 92 percent, with 99 percent of eligible voters casting ballots. Many voters, however, say they did not bother to vote because they felt the outcome was a foregone conclusion. Nyi Nyi, an office worker, stated about the vote, "That is the least of my concerns. I wake up every morning planning where to get water,

RESIDENTS OF A TOWN WEST OF RANGOON CAST THEIR VOTES IN THE constitutional referendum in May 2008.

and when to start queuing [standing in line] for gasoline." Others claimed that government officials voted in their places, telling them only after the vote that their ballots had been sent in.

Two weeks after Cyclone Nargis, Than Shwe finally stepped out of the shadows. He toured a refugee camp, and state television showed him patting babies and shaking hands as refugees bowed to him. Yet this contrived photo opportunity could not mask the people's growing anger. As more aid workers and other foreigners were granted visas to enter Burma, the survivors were quick to voice their discontent to them, usually with a guarantee of anonymity. One villager spoke of the day government officials came to his village with television cameras and handed out supplies. As soon as the cameras were turned off, though, the villager reported, "in 20 minutes it all stopped and the officials said there was going to be no more food and told us to go home."

By this time, the UN estimated that 1.5 million survivors had been severely affected by the storm, meaning that they had lost homes, family members, or livelihoods. Countries from Australia to Vietnam had sent donations of funds, food, supplies, and workers to help out. Volunteers from member countries of ASEAN had been permitted to enter Burma, and on May 22, the secretary-general of the UN, Ban Ki-moon, visited the country. He spoke with Prime Minister Thein Sein and Foreign Minister Nyan Win and finally with Than Shwe. The secretary-general pledged the support of the international community to the Burmese, saying, "I praise the will, resilience and the courage of the people of Myanmar. I bring a message of hope." He toured the delta region by helicopter, shaken by the destruction he saw. By the end of his visit, the government had agreed to allow in aid and aid workers, though it would not permit U.S. or European warships carrying supplies to dock.

UN SECRETARY-GENERAL BAN KI-MOON *(SECOND FROM LEFT)* **VISITS A REFUGEE** camp housing thousands left homeless by Cyclone Nargis. He met with Burmese officials to convince the government to accept international aid.

By the end of May, the UN's estimate of Burma's dead had climbed to 134,000, with more than 2 million survivors facing hunger and homelessness. As the weeks passed, more foreign aid workers were granted visas and aid continued to trickle in, both officially and unofficially. The junta finally permitted helicopters to fly upriver to help those most isolated by the storm. Aid groups continued to distribute what they could bring in. However, in early June, the U.S. warships that had come laden with contributions of food and supplies were forced to turn and leave. Reports from inside Burma showed roads lined with thousands of homeless and hungry men, women, and children. Footage showed monasteries overflowing with displaced people, as the monks did their best to feed and clothe them with the few supplies available.

> *"I don't want to say much but the monks are doing all the cleaning up. I've seen about 200 monks in Kemmedine township, and the same number in Sanchaung township, clearing the fallen trees and leading work parties. The USDA [the civilian arm of the military junta] have turned up but they're not really doing anything—they're just standing around."*
>
> –Burmese woman in Rangoon, 2008

During this time, the date on which Aung San Suu Kyi's house arrest was supposed to end—May 25—came and went. Without fanfare, Than Shwe extended her sentence for another year. The UN, EU, and the U.S. government, each concerned with trying to help the cyclone victims, chose not to focus on Aung San Suu Kyi's situation. They realized that trying to force conditions on the junta would only further endanger the starving Burmese by closing off the limited channels of international assistance. Than Shwe and his generals knew they had the upper hand, and they did not appear to care that their power was the result of the world's concern for the suffering of their people. Rather than weakening the regime, the storm had strengthened the junta's hold on its ravaged country.

WHAT NEXT

THAN SHWE TURNED SEVENTY-FIVE IN 2008, and reports hinted that he was very ill. It seems likely that the bulldog of Burma's junta will be gone soon. But in what direction will the country turn next?

Burma's past is one of nearly endless conflict and warfare. Since the ninth century, when the Nanzhao raced down from the mountains of China, ethnic groups within the country have been at war. The junta currently recognizes 135 ethnic groups. At least 20 of these groups have armed dissident operations. In the past several years, the junta has signed cease-fire agreements with the majority of ethnic opposition groups, but these pacts have not prevented armed skirmishes from taking place. In addition, many ethnic minority groups have refused to sign agreements. The Karen National Union (KNU), the Shan State Army, the Chin National Front, the Karenni National Progressive Party (KNPP), and several

FOR BURMA?

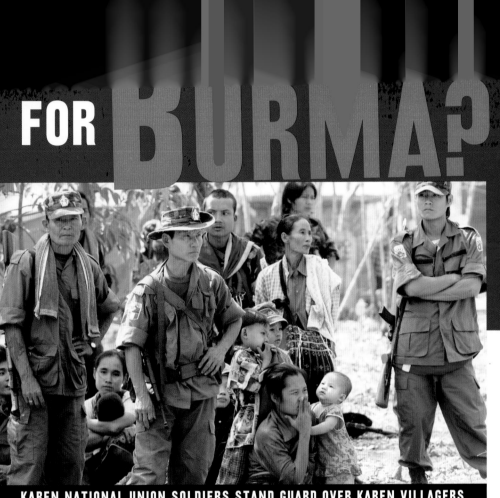

KAREN NATIONAL UNION SOLDIERS STAND GUARD OVER KAREN VILLAGERS in south central Burma. Karen civilians fear that the Burmese army will destroy their homes or take them away to forced labor camps.

Rohingya groups have not participated in the cease-fire. Even those groups that are part of the cease-fire agreements are subject to violence and repression by government forces.

The Karen have been fighting the junta for years. In the 1970s, the government began launching offensives against many ethnic minority groups. Since the Karen live on the Thai border, many villagers fled to Thailand, where nearly eighty thousand live in refugee camps. The Karen National Union fights against the human rights abuses and alleged "ethnic cleansing," a deliberate attempt to kill off the entire ethnic group, by the junta. Since many of the Karen are Christians, they also claim they are enduring religious persecution by the government.

"Even though we are civilians, the military treats us like their enemy."
—Karen refugee living in Thailand, 1999

The Karenni too have resisted the regime for decades. They founded the Karenni National Progressive Party in 1957 to spearhead their efforts. In 1995 they established a cease-fire with the junta, but it collapsed almost immediately. The KNPP has accused the junta of ethnic cleansing.

The Kachin claim discrimination by the junta because of their Christian religion. They have also endured forced labor and land confiscations. The Muslim Rohingya have endured even greater discrimination. They are required to obtain a permit before they can marry, and they must apply for a pass to move outside their villages, even for health care. The army has forced them to work without pay and has taken their land.

MEMBERS OF THE SHAN STATE ARMY SING THE SHAN NATIONAL ANTHEM
during a memorial service for Shan people killed in the resistance movement.

The Shan have suffered forced relocation by the junta since the 1990s. More than 120,000 villagers were forcibly moved before 2002, and many were required to do hard labor for the military. Two hundred thousand live in relocation sites and refugee camps in Thailand.

The Mon have had much of their farmland confiscated by the military. Many fled to Thailand, where they lived in refugee camps. However, in 1996, the Thai government forced the refugees back into Burma. Few of them returned to their villages, as they had no homes or land left. More than forty thousand Mon remain in hiding or in camps.

In addition to ethnic dissident groups within Burma, a government in exile, led by Prime Minister Sein Win, includes many of the exiled members of the NLD. The NLD itself is active within Burma. A coalition of exiled opposition groups called the National Council-

LEADERS OF THE 88 GENERATION STUDENTS ARRIVE AT MARTYRS' DAY celebrations in Rangoon in 2007. Martyrs' Day commemorates the assassination of Aung San and six other members of the Anti-Fascist People's Freedom League.

Union of Burma and a group called the 88 Generation Students, a pro-democracy movement, work outside the country. Dozens of other ethnic and political opposition groups are active as well. How can such a politically and ethnically fractured country possibly come together to create a government that can run efficiently and without violence?

Over half the country is ethnically Bamar, and the national hero Aung San was Bamar. Some see the main conflict in the country as between the Bamars, who want democracy, and the military establishment. However, many of the ethnic minorities fear that even democracy will leave them out of the governing of the country and will not ensure the safety and prosperity of their people. As one

Karen said to a Bamar at a meeting in Washington, D.C., "We don't want your people to rule our people."

Even if Aung San Suu Kyi were released from house arrest and allowed to take on the leadership role that many Burmese long to give her, some groups of ethnic minorities would still view her and any government she established with great mistrust. She feels strongly that a democratic government in Burma would have to include a coalition of different ethnic groups, stating, "What we need is a system of a federal nature that takes into consideration all the aspirations of different nationalities."

If, as is more likely, the junta were to continue to rule after Than Shwe, the dictator's second-in-command, Vice Senior General Maung Aye, appears to be in line to take his place. Maung Aye is chief of the army. Rumors hint that he is out of favor with Than Shwe, however. If Maung Aye did not take over, the next in line is General Thura Shwe Mann, who is well liked by the troops and has earned commendations for bravery. (*Thura* is a title meaning "brave.") Like Than Shwe, Thura Shwe Mann is relatively unknown and keeps to himself. His reputation is, as yet, untarnished by human rights violations. He is in his late fifties, as opposed to Maung Aye's late sixties and Than Shwe's late seventies, so he might have decades to rule the country.

GENERAL THURA SHWE MANN is the joint chief of staff of the Burmese armed forces.

Some who are familiar with Burma and the junta fear that if the ruling group shows any weakness, it will give the Chinese a reason to step in and take over. China's fast-growing need for energy makes Burma's vast reserves of natural gas a strong lure, and China and Burma have had close relations for decades. Whether China would risk the international disapproval such a move would create worldwide is questionable. But Burma, though isolated and relatively unknown to much of the world, remains a vital source of natural resources and an important gateway into the rest of Southeast Asia. Thant Myint-U, the grandson of U Thant, speaking in 2008 about the Burma-China relationship, said, "The most important development of the last 20 years is . . . the opening up to China. I think the life of the ordinary Burmese

THANT MYINT-U *(LEFT)* SPOKE ABOUT THE HISTORY OF BURMA AT A UNITED Nations event in 2007. He is known for his books, *The River of Lost Footsteps* and *The Making of Modern Burma.*

people in 10 or 20 years from now will depend much more on how that relationship evolves than almost anything else."

An article in an August 2008 *New Yorker* detailed reporter George Packer's trip through parts of post-cyclone Burma. He observed the Burmese struggling to feed themselves and to rebuild their destroyed homes. Though they worked without help from government officials, they still hoped that in the future, things would change for the better. Many long for democracy, but others, though they despise the military junta, believe that if the country were to begin to move toward democracy, the military would have to be a part of it. Packer writes, "Having strangled civil society, hollowed out the bureaucracy, and locked up the political opposition, the Army can rightly claim to be the only institution capable of running things."

"The generals don't care what the rest of the world thinks about them, because they don't think about the rest of the world. What they care about is their financial and physical security."

–Western diplomat in Rangoon, describing the junta's foreign policy to George Packer in 2008

Some Burmese with whom Packer spoke felt that increased interaction with the outside world would help bring about change. They believe that boycotts against Burma have been counterproductive.

Sanctions have served only to increase poverty and isolate the country still further and have given Than Shwe the freedom to do what he will with the country. Thant Myint-U said, "If there's one thing that's fueled Burma's many problems over the last half century, it's been its isolation." But Burma's isolation has decreased in recent years as politicians and celebrities from the United States and elsewhere have begun to make the country a popular cause.

Speaking for the U.S. administration in 2008, First Lady Laura Bush condemned Aung San Suu Kyi's house arrest. From a different political perspective, musicians Sheryl Crow and Jackson Browne, comedians Sarah Silverman and Jim Carrey, and actors Ellen Page, Dustin Hoffman, Angelina Jolie, and Brad Pitt are among those who

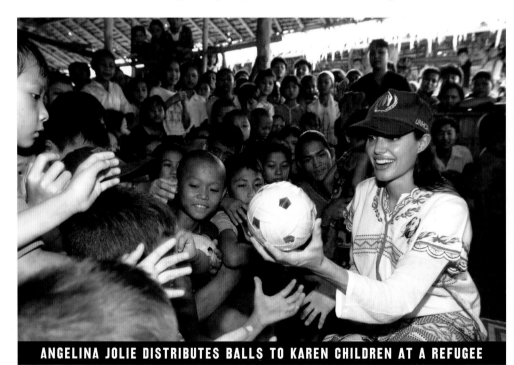

ANGELINA JOLIE DISTRIBUTES BALLS TO KAREN CHILDREN AT A REFUGEE camp on the border between Burma and Thailand. Jolie toured the area in 2002 as a goodwill ambassador for the United Nations High Commissioner for Refugees.

have called for freedom and democracy in the country. The Dalai Lama, the exiled spiritual head of Tibet, has also extended his support to the democratic movement in Burma.

The Burmese, however, know that a change in their government will probably not come as a result of outside influence. They are aware that freedom and an end to repression must come from within. One relief worker voiced this belief, saying, "When I was younger, I hoped and waited for outside help to come to our country and liberate it. Now I realize that we have to rely on ourselves."

WHO'S WHO?

ANAWRAHTA (?–1077): Anawrahta, also known as Aniruddha, was king of the Bamars from 1044 to 1077. He was born in Pagan. He united Burma for the first time, conquering the Mon people and bringing Buddhism to the Burmese. During his reign and those of his descendants, the Burmese built thousands of pagodas that still dot the landscape.

AUNG SAN (1915–1947): Aung San was born in Natmauk and became politically active while attending the University of Rangoon. During World War II, he fought alongside the Japanese at first, but he realized Burma could not achieve independence under Japan's influence and worked with the Allies to help drive the Japanese from Burma. After helping to work out an agreement for Burmese independence from Britain, he was assassinated in July 1947.

AUNG SAN SUU KYI (1945–): Daughter of Aung San, Aung San Suu Kyi was born in Rangoon and educated in Burma, India, and Great Britain. She married an Englishman and worked in Bhutan but moved back to Burma in 1988, when her mother had a stroke. After the uprising of 8-8-88, the government placed her under house arrest for her criticism of the military regime. A leader of the pro-democracy National League for Democracy, she has been held under house arrest for much of the last two decades. In 1991 she was awarded the Nobel Peace Prize.

BAYINNAUNG (CA. 1515–1581): Bayinnaung conquered the Mon people of southern Burma and proclaimed himself king in 1551. His capital was the city of Pegu. In 1554 he marched against Siam, which the Burmese then ruled for the next fifteen years. Bayinnaung built many pagodas and helped spread Buddhism throughout his kingdom.

IBRAHIM GAMBARI (1944–): Ibrahim Gambari was born in Nigeria and received degrees from the London School of Economics and Columbia University in New York. He served as permanent representative to the United Nations from Nigeria and joined the UN Secretariat in 1999. He was made undersecretary general in 2005 and since 2007 has been working closely with the secretary-general as a special adviser on Iraq and other issues, including UN relations with Burma.

KHIN NYUNT (1939–): Born in Kyauktan, Khin Nyunt is an ethnic Chinese who rose through the ranks of the Burmese military. He was appointed chief of intelligence in 1983 and became the secretary of the State Law and Order Restoration Council and then prime minister in 2003. He announced the government's seven-step road map to democracy, and many considered him a moderate voice within the government. In 2004 he was officially "permitted to retire," and shortly afterward, the government charged him with corruption. In 2005 he was sentenced to forty-four years in prison, which he is currently serving under house arrest.

MAUNG MAUNG (1925–1994): Maung Maung fought alongside the Burmese nationalists during World War II and then studied law at the University of Rangoon. He was admitted to the bar in London, England, and taught in Utrecht, the Netherlands, and at Yale University. After Ne Win's coup in 1962, Maung Maung became a Supreme Court justice and a member of the BSPP central committee. When Ne Win stepped down in 1988, Maung Maung was declared president. He remained in power for only one month, until the SLORC took power.

MINDON (1814–1878): Mindon was king of Burma from 1853 until his death in 1878. He was born in Amarapura and took the throne from his half brother, who had been at war with Britain. Under his reign, Burma's culture flowered. He was a devout Buddhist. He moved the capital to Mandalay, made temporary peace with the British (though they continued to occupy part of the country), and modernized the Burmese economy. However, after his brother and successor was assassinated, he did not designate an heir to the throne. When Mindon died, his son Prince Thibaw, who was young and unqualified, became king.

NE WIN (1911–2002): Born Shu Maung when Burma was a British Indian province, Ne Win was born near Prome and educated at the University of Rangoon. He became involved in politics before World War II and, with Aung San, formed the Burma Independence Army, fighting first with and then against the Japanese. He became commander of the Burmese armed forces after the war and overturned Prime Minister U Nu's government in 1962. He controlled the government until 1988, and even after the State Law and Order Restoration Council took over, many assumed he worked behind the scenes to run the state.

U NU (1907–1995): U Nu was born in Wakema, the son of a politician. At the University of Rangoon, U Nu was involved in the 1936 students' strike protesting the British occupation of Burma and was expelled from the university for his role in the protests. He served in the Japanese-controlled government during World War II but secretly worked against the Japanese. After Aung San's assassination, U Nu became independent Burma's first prime minister. He helped the country maintain neutrality and strengthened the Buddhist influence within Burma. In 1958 Ne Win's forces removed him from office, but he was reelected. In 1962 Ne Win again took over the reigns of government, this time imprisoning U Nu for several years. In 1969 U Nu fled Burma, fearing he would be imprisoned again. He established a government in exile, not returning until after the uprising of 8-8-88. The SLORC saw him as a threat and placed him under house arrest for three years. He remained in seclusion until his death.

SAW MAUNG (1928–1997): Saw Maung was born in Mandalay. He joined the army in 1949 and was a supporter of Ne Win. Ne Win made him chairman of the Burma Socialist Program Party after the 1962 coup. He became a general in 1988, and after the SLORC coup of 1988, he became a senior general and chairman in charge of the military government. After the elections of 1990, he refused to allow the winning NLD members of parliament to take their seats. The ensuing protests by the Burmese weakened his hold on the country, and in 1992, he stepped down, citing health reasons. He died in July 1997.

THAN SHWE (1933–): Than Shwe was born in Kyaukse and joined the army when he was twenty. He rose through the ranks and became a ruling member of the Burma Socialist Program Party under Ne Win. After the uprising of 8-8-88, he was made one of the government's cabinet members under Saw Maung. When Saw Maung retired in 1992, Than

Shwe, then a senior general, took over the reins of government. He has ruled as dictator since 1992.

U THANT (1909–1974): U Thant was born in the Irrawaddy Delta and attended the University of Rangoon, where he met Aung San and U Nu. He worked as a teacher until Burma achieved independence. When U Nu became prime minister, he sent U Thant as Burma's representative to the United Nations, his post from 1952 until 1961, when he was elected secretary-general. He remained in that position for a decade. After his death in 1974, his body was flown back to Rangoon, where university students seized his coffin and buried it on the grounds of the university. Not long afterward, the police seized his body and reburied it near the Shwedagon Pagoda, sealing the tomb with concrete. The government declared martial law to subdue the protests that their action sparked.

THIBAW (1858–1916): Born in Mandalay, Thibaw was a younger son of King Mindon. As king, he allowed corruption to flourish within his government and in the business community. Thibaw enacted a trade treaty with France, infuriating the British. He then accused a British company of cheating the Burmese government out of tax money and demanded a huge fine. The British asked that the case be reconsidered. Thibaw refused to respond, and the British used the situation as an excuse to annex the rest of Burma, deposing the king. Thibaw remained in exile in India until his death.

WIN TIN (1930–): Win Tin began working as an editor while still in college and became a newspaper editor during the time Ne Win controlled the government. After writing an article critical of Ne Win's Burmese Way to Socialism, he was dismissed from his newspaper job and became a freelance reporter. He was arrested by the SLORC in 1989 and imprisoned for antigovernment activities. Until his inexplicable release in September of 2008, he was the world's longest-serving prisoner of conscience. He suffered in prison from debilitating spinal problems and heart ailments but was rarely allowed to see a doctor. He has received awards from UNESCO and the World Association of Newspapers for his defense of freedom of the press.

TIMELINE

CA. 9000 B.C.   Earliest known people settle in Burma.

CA. 1500 B.C.   The Mon people establish their first kingdom in eastern Burma.

CA. A.D. 100   The Pyu people establish several city-states in central and northern Burma.

800S   The Bamars establish the First Burmese Empire, with its capital at Pagan. The Nanzhao move into the Irrawaddy Valley.

1057   King Anawrahta defeats the Mon.

1287   The Mongols defeat the Burmese.

1558   King Bayinnaung establishes the Second Burmese Empire.

1755   King Alaungpaya founds the Third Burmese Empire.

1824   The British win the First Anglo-Burmese War.

1852   The British capture Rangoon in the Second Anglo-Burmese War.

1857   King Mindon establishes the capital at Mandalay.

1885   The British make Burma part of India at the end of the Third Anglo-Burmese War.

1937   Britain separates Burma from India, allowing it its own constitution and legislature.

1942   Japan invades Burma.

1945   Burmese and Allied troops defeat the Japanese.

1947   Aung San is assassinated.

1948   Burma wins independence from British rule. U Nu becomes prime minister.

1962   General Ne Win seizes power in a coup.

1974   Ne Win proclaims Burma a Socialist republic.

1988   Protesters march against the military government. Soldiers kill hundreds of antigovernment protesters. The State Law and Order Restoration Council takes control of the government.

1989   The government places Aung San Suu Kyi under house arrest.

1990   In national elections, the National League for Democracy wins a majority of seats, but their representatives are not allowed to sit in parliament.

1991   Aung San Suu Kyi is awarded the Nobel Peace Prize.

1992   General Than Shwe takes power.

1997   The SLORC renames itself the State Peace and Development Council (SPDC).

2003   Aung San Suu Kyi is arrested and put back under house arrest. The United States bans trade with Burma.

2005   The government moves the capital to Naypyidaw.

2007   Burmese monks lead an antigovernment uprising. The regime retaliates with violence. The United States and EU strengthen sanctions against Burma.

2008   Cyclone Nargis hits Burma. Tens of thousands of people die. Aung San Suu Kyi's house arrest is extended. A referendum calling for elections and adopting a new constitution passes.

2009   The United Nations states that almost one-tenth of Burmese people live below the food poverty line. UN Special Envoy Ibrahim Gambari met with Aung San Suu Kyi and NLD members to discuss the upcoming 2010 elections.

GLOSSARY

alms: in Burma, donations given to monks or nuns. Giving alms is believed to confer spiritual merit on the giver.

amnesty: a legal pardon for political offenses

ASEAN: the Association of Southeast Asian Nations, a group consisting of ten nations that was formed in 1967 to promote peaceful cooperation and economic development

black market: the illegal buying and selling of goods, usually at hugely inflated prices

BSPP: the Burma Socialist Program Party; Ne Win's political party formed after the coup of 1962

Buddhism: a religion based on the teachings of Siddhartha Gautama (the Buddha) in the sixth century B.C. that holds that life consists of suffering created by desire and that spiritual enlightenment can end the cycle of birth and death

dissident: someone who disagrees with or rebels against the government

GDP: gross domestic product; the value of goods and services produced within a nation's border in a given time

house arrest: the confinement of a person who has been arrested to his or her house

nationalize: to bring the ownership of industry and land under government control

nirvana: in Buddhism, freedom from the cycle of birth and death

NLD: the National League for Democracy, the Burmese political party headed by Aung San Suu Kyi

ratify: to approve or sanction officially

ration: to limit provisions or food during a shortage

relocation: the forcible movement of people from their homes to another location

sanctions: penalties for violations of international law

SLORC: the State Law and Order Restoration Council, the name given to the government by the military junta after its takeover in 1988

Socialist: an economic system with state or worker ownership of production

SPDC: the State Peace and Development Council, the name given to the government by Than Shwe in 1997

Tatmadaw: the Burmese armed forces under Than Shwe

tribunal: a military court

vinaya: the rules of Buddhism, originally passed down orally from the Buddha

SOURCE NOTES

8 Seth Mydans, "Police Clash with Monks in Myanmar," *New York Times*, July 26, 2007, http://www.nytimes.com/2007/09/26/world/asia/26cnd-myanmar.html?scp=1&sq=police%20clash%20with%20monks%20in%20myanmar&st=cse (February 3, 2009).

9 IBMC. "The Metta Sutta," *International Buddhist Meditation Center*, n.d., http://www.urbandharma.org/ibmc/ibmc1/metta.html (February 3, 2009).

17 Thant Myint-U, *The River of Lost Footsteps* (New York: Farrar Straus & Giroux, 2006), 52.

23 Marco Polo, *The Travels of Marco Polo*, vol. 1, May 22, 2004, http://www.gutenberg.org/files/12410/12410-8.txt (February 3, 2009).

25 Gaspero Balbi, *Voyage to Pegu, and Observations There, Circa 1583, SOAS Bulletin of Burma Research* 1, no. 2 (Autumn 2003): 30.

26 D. G. E. Hall, *Europe and Burma* (London: Oxford University Press, 1945), 66–67.

27 William Hunter, *A Concise Account of the Kingdom of Pegu, SOAS Bulletin of Burma Research* 3, no. 1 (Spring 2005): 190.

29 John James Snodgrass. *Narrative of the Burmese War* (London: John Murray, Albemarle-Street, 1827), 6.

38 Aung San, "An Address to the Anglo-Burmans," *Aung San of Burma,* December 8, 1946, n.d., http://www.aungsan.com/Anglo_Burmans.htm (February 3, 2009).

44 Revolutionary Council of the Union of Burma, *The Burmese Way to Socialism*, 3rd ed., Burma Socialist Programme Party, April 28, 1962, n.d., http://burmalibrary.org/docs/The_Burmese_Way_to_Socialism.htm (February 3, 2009).

49 Ferrara, Federico, "Why Regimes Create Disorder: Hobbes's Dilemma during a

Rangoon Summer," *Journal of Conflict Resolution* 47, no. 3 (June 2003): 313–314.

56 Aung San Suu Kyi, *Freedom from Fear and Other Writings*, ed. Michael Aris (New York: Viking, 1991), 199.

61 Associated Press, "Myanmar's Fate Lies in the Hands of Junta 'Bulldog,'" *MSNBC*, October 22, 2007, http://www.msnbc.msn .com/id/21103992/ (February 3, 2009).

63 Ed Cropley, "Than Shwe, Myanmar Junta's 'Old Fox,'" *Reuters*, October 3, 2007, http://www.reuters.com/ article/topNews/ idUSBKK29328420071003 (February 3, 2009).

64 Aung San Suu Kyi, "Nobel Lecture," *Nobel Foundation*, 1991, http://nobelprize.org/ nobel_prizes/peace/laureates/ 1991/kyi-acceptance.html (February 3, 2009).

65 Aung San Suu Kyi, *Freedom from Fear,* 183.

67 Ian Mackinnon, "Burma's Leader Urges Citizens to 'Crush Destructive Elements,'"

Guardian, March 28, 2008, http://www.guardian.co.uk/ world/2008/mar/28/burma/ print (February 3, 2009).

71 Kenneth Denby, "Inside Than Shwe's Jungle Fortress," *Times Online*, October 15, 2007, http://timesonline.typepad .com/times_tokyo_weblog/ 2007/10/inside-than-shw.html (February 3, 2009).

72 Associated Press, "Myanmar's Fate."

72 Cropley, "Junta's 'Old Fox.'"

72 Ibid.

72 *New Internationalist*, "Than Shwe," September 2005, http:// www.newint.org/columns/ worldbeaters/2005/09/01/ than_shwe/ (February 3, 2009).

72 Kerry Brown, "Paranoid, Insular, and Inept, the Junta Has No Plan B," *Guardian,* September 28, 2007, http:// www.guardian.co.uk/ commentisfree/2007/sep/28/ comment.burma/print (February 3, 2009).

73 *Irrawaddy*, "Than Shwe Watch," March 27, 2006, http://www

.irrawaddy.org/print_article.
php?art_id=5597 (February 3,
2009).

73 Ibid, November 12, 2006.

77 Naw Paw Aye, "Then I Never
Saw Her Again," *Internally
Displaced People's Stories and
Experiences,* 2005, http://www.
kwekalu.net/photojournal1/
idp/idpstory1.html (February
3, 2009).

83 HRW, "The Monk's Story," *Human
Rights Watch Report: "They
Came and Destroyed Our Village
Again,"* June 9, 2005, http://
www.hrw.org/en/node/11703/
(February 2, 2009).

84 Naw Paw Aye, "Then I Never
Saw Her Again."

85 Martin Smith, *Ethnic Groups
in Burma: Development,
Democracy, and Human
Rights* (London: Anti-Slavery
International, 1994), 87,
available online at http://
www.burmalibrary.org/docs3/
Ethnic_Groups_in_Burma-ocr
.pdf (February 3, 2009).

85 Ibid., 88.

88 Kate McGeown, "Life under

Burma's Military Regime," *BBC,*
June 15, 2006, http://news.bbc.
co.uk/2/hi/asia-pacific/5071966.
stm (February 3, 2009).

92 George Packer, "Letter from
Rangoon: Drowning," *New
Yorker,* August 25, 2008, 50.

97 Embassy of the Union
of Myanmar, *National
Environmental Policy of the
Union of Myanmar,* March
26, 2006, http://www.
mewashingtondc
.com/environment.htm
(February 3, 2009).

100 A. Lin Neumann, "Burma under
Pressure," *CPJ,* February 2002,
http://www.cpj.org/Briefings/
2002/Burma_feb02/Burma_
feb02.html (February 3, 2009).

102 Ibid.

104 AAPP, *The Darkness We
See: Torture in Burma's
Interrogation Centers and
Prisons* (Mae Sot, Thailand:
Assistance Association for
Political Prisoners [Burma]),
December 2005, 31, http://
www.aappb.org/tortour
_report.pdf (February 3, 2009).

105 Ibid., 43.

105 Ibid., 59.

107 Ibid., 92.

113 Ibrahim Gambari, "We Don't Do 'Regime Change,'" *Newsweek*, January 19, 2008, http://www.newsweek.com/ id/96344/output/print (February 3, 2009).

113 Ibid.

117 BBC, "Q and A: Protests in Burma," *BBC News*, October 2, 2007, http://news.bbc.co.uk/1/ hi/world/asia-pacific/7010202 .stm (February 3, 2009).

119 HRW, "Crackdown Bloodier Than Government Admits," *Human Rights Watch,* (December 5, 2007), http://www.hrw.org/ en/news/2007/12/06/burma -crackdown-bloodier- government-admits (February 4, 2009).

120 AFP, "Myanmar's Suu Kyi Says 'Time for Healing' After Junta Meeting," November 8, 2007, *AFP,* 2009, http:// afp.google.com/article/ ALeqM5iTYCIwEISNvroeC _sRmFxCH4VqFg (February 3, 2009).

121 Seth Mydans, "Constitutional Referendum Still the Priority for Myanmar Leaders," *International Herald Tribune,* May 9, 2008, http://www.iht .com/articles/2008/05/09/ asia/myanmar.php (February 3, 2009).

121 Lalit K. Jha, "UNSC Issues Presidential Statement on Burma," *Irrawaddy,* May 3, 2008, http://www.irrawaddy.org/ print_article.php?art_id=11750 (February 3, 2009).

122 Ibid.

124 BBC, "Burma Cyclone: Eyewitness Reports," *BBC News,* May 6, 2008, http:// news.bbc.co.uk/2/hi/asia -pacific/7383821.stm (February 4, 2009).

126 CNN, "Cyclone Overshadows Myanmar Referendum," *CNN,* May 10, 2008, http://www .cnn.com/2008/WORLD/ asiapcf/05/09/myanmar.vote .ap/index.html (July 22, 2008).

127 *New York Times,* "2 Weeks after Cyclone, Burmese Leader Pays First Visit to Refugees," May 17, 2008.

127 John Heilprin. "UN Chief Tours Still-Flooded Myanmar Delta," *Associated Press,* May 22, 2008, http://abcnews.go.com/ International/wireStory?id =4906929 (February 3, 2009).

129 BBC, "Burma Cyclone."

132 Amnesty International, "The Kayin (Karen) State: Militarization and Human Rights," *Amnesty International,* June 1, 1999, http://www .amnesty.org/en/library/ asset/ASA16/012/1999/en/ dom-ASA160121999en.html (February 3, 2009).

135 Nai Ong Mon, "The Future of Burma," *Monland Restoration Council,* n.d., http://www.mrc -usa.org/Self_future_of_burma .htm (February 3, 2009).

135 *UNESCO,* "Aung San Suu Kyi: 'We've Got to Move Forward,'" *New Courier,* April 2003, http:// portal.unesco.org/es/ev.php -URL_ID=10384&URL_DO=DO _TOPIC&URL_SECTION=201 .html (February 3, 2009).

136 Seth Mydans, "Exiles Try to Rekindle Hopes for Change in Myanmar," *New York Times,* August 6, 2008.

137 Packer, "Letter from Rangoon," 53.

137 Ibid.

138 Ibid.

139 Ibid., 55.

SELECTED BIBLIOGRAPHY

AAPP. *The Darkness We See: Torture in Burma's Interrogation Centers and Prisons*. Mae Sot, Thailand: Assistance Association for Political Prisoners (Burma), December 2005. http://www.aappb.org/tortour_report.pdf (February 2, 2009).

Associated Press. "Myanmar's Fate Lies in the Hands of Junta 'Bulldog.'" *MSNBC*. October 22, 2007. http://www.msnbc.msn.com/id/21103992/ (February 2, 2009).

Aung San Suu Kyi. *Freedom from Fear and Other Writings*. Edited by Michael Aris. New York: Viking, 1991.

Brown, Kerry. "Paranoid, Insular, and Inept, the Junta Has No Plan B." *Guardian*, September 28, 2007. http://www.guardian.co.uk/commentisfree/2007/sep/28/comment.burma/print (February 2, 2009).

Clements, Alan. *The Voice of Hope*. New York: Seven Stories Press, 1997.

Cropley, Ed. "Than Shwe, Myanmar Junta's 'Old Fox.'" *Reuters*. October 3, 2007. http://www.reuters.com/article/topNews/idUSBKK29328420071003 (February 2, 2009).

HRW. "The Monk's Story." *Human Rights Watch Report: "They Came and Destroyed Our Village Again."* June 9, 2005, http://www.hrw.org/en/node/11703/ (February 2, 2009).

Humphries, Richard. *Frontier Mosaic*. Bangkok, Thailand: Orchid Press, 2007.

Irrawaddy. "Than Shwe Watch." December 3, 2008. http://www.irrawaddy.org/print_article.php?art_id=5597 (February 2, 2009).

Mydans, Seth. "Police Clash with Monks in Myanmar." *New York Times*, July 26, 2007. http://www.nytimes.com/2007/09/26/world/asia/26cnd-myanmar.html?scp=1&sq=police%20clash%20with%20monks%20in%20myanmar&st=cse (February 2, 2009).

Nai Ong Mon. "The Future of Burma." *Monland Restoration Council.* N.d. http://www.mrc-usa.org/Self_future_of_burma.htm (July 22, 2008).

Nash, Manning. *The Golden Road to Modernity.* New York: John Wiley & Son, 1965.

Packer, George. "Letter from Rangoon: Drowning." *New Yorker*, August 25, 2008, 40–55.

Roycee, Alden T., editor. *Burma in Turmoil.* New York: Nova Science Publishers, 2008.

Smith, Martin. *Ethnic Groups in Burma: Development, Democracy, and Human Rights.* London: Anti-Slavery International, 1994. Available online at http://www.burmalibrary.org/docs3/Ethnic_Groups_in _Burma-ocr.pdf (February 2, 2009).

Soe Myint. *Burma File.* Singapore: Marshall Cavendish Academic, 2004.

Thant Myint-U. *The River of Lost Footsteps.* New York: Farrar Straus & Giroux, 2006.

Tucker, Shelby. *Burma: The Curse of Independence.* London: Pluto Press, 2001.

Wallechinsky, David. *The World's 20 Worst Living Dictators.* New York: HarperCollins, 2006.

Wintle, Justin. *Perfect Hostage.* London: Random House, 2007.

FURTHER READING AND WEBSITES

BOOKS

Behnke, Alison. *China in Pictures.* Minneapolis: Twenty-First Century Books, 2003. This book provides an overview of China, Burma's Communist neighbor and trade partner.

Hasday, Judy L. *Aung San Suu Kyi.* New York: Chelsea House Publishers, 2007. This recent biography follows Aung San Suu Kyi's work toward democratic reform and civil rights in Burma.

Khng, Pauline. *Myanmar.* Milwaukee: Gareth Stevens Publishing, 2000. This book for young readers describes Burma's history and culture.

Pascal Khoo Thwe. *From the Land of Green Ghosts.* New York: HarperCollins, 2002. This book for older readers tells the story of a young man from the Kayan ethnic group who becomes a guerilla fighter against Than Shwe's regime.

Saw Myat Yin. *Myanmar.* Tarrytown, NY: Marshall Cavendish, 2002. This entry in the CultureShock! series gives a concise overview of the culture and history of Burma, along with extensive travel information.

Smith, Roland. *Elephant Run.* New York: Hyperion, 2007. When the Japanese invade Burma during World War II, a British boy and his Burman friend must rescue their loved ones from a jungle prison camp.

Stewart, Whitney. *Aung San Suu Kyi.* Minneapolis: Twenty-First Century Books, 1997. This biography of Aung San Suu Kyi draws on personal interviews with the Burmese leader and those around her.

Streissguth, Tom. *Myanmar in Pictures.* Minneapolis: Twenty-First Century Books, 2008. This young-adult book provides an overview of the land, history, government, people, cultural life, and economy of Myanmar.

Tan, Amy. *Saving Fish from Drowning.* New York: Putnam, 2005. A group of Americans on an art tour of Asia fall in with Burmese villagers hiding from Tan Shwe's government.

WEBSITES

The Assistance Association for Political Prisoners, Burma
> http://www.aappb.org/pp.html
> This site archives information on Burmese political prisoners.

Aung San Suu Kyi's Site
> http://www.dassk.com/index.php
> This site is devoted to information about Aung San Suu Kyi, with biographical information, up-to-date notices about her actions, and links to other sites about Burma and the Burmese.

The Burma Campaign, UK
> http://www.burmacampaign.org.uk
> This British site aims to restore human rights to Burma through government lobbying and dissemination of information.

The Burma Library
> http://www.burmalibrary.org/show.php?cat=496&lo=d&sl=0
> This site contains original documents pertaining to Burmese history, culture, and politics.

Doctors Without Borders
> http://www.doctorswithoutborders.org/news/country.cfm?id=2296
> A section of the site of Doctors Without Borders, an international medical charity, is dedicated to detailing their work in Burma, through articles and podcasts.

Irrawaddy
> http://www.irrawaddy.org
> This is the site of a newspaper run by Burmese exiles in Thailand that details events within and outside the country.

Visual Geography Series: Myanmar
> http://www.vgsbooks.com
> The home page of the Visual Geography Series® links to sites with additional information and late-breaking news about Myanmar.

INDEX

AUTHOR BIOGRAPHY

Diane Zahler studied medieval history in college. She has written textbooks for students in kindergarten through grade twelve in history, language arts, and literature. She is the coauthor of *Test Your Cultural Literacy,* a quiz book; *The Twenty-First Century Guide to Improving Your Writing;* and *The Black Death.* She lives in Wassaic, New York.

PHOTO ACKNOWLEDGMENTS